Harvard Publications in Music

1. The Complete Works of Anthony Holborne, edited by Masakata Kanazawa. Volume I: Music for Lute and Bandora.
2. The Symphonies of G. B. Sammartini, edited by Bathia Churgin. Volume I: The Early Symphonies.

3–4. The Lute Music of Francesco Canova da Milano (1497–1543), edited by Arthur J. Ness. Volumes I and II (2 volumes in 1).

5. The Complete Works of Anthony Holborne, edited by Masakata Kanazawa. Volume II: Music for Cittern.
6. The Operas of Alessandro Scarlatti, Donald Jay Grout, General Editor. Volume I: Eraclea, edited by Donald Jay Grout.
7. The Operas of Alessandro Scarlatti, Donald Jay Grout, General Editor. Volume II: Marco Attilio Regolo, edited by Joscelyn Godwin.
8. The Operas of Alessandro Scarlatti, Donald Jay Grout, General Editor. Volume III: Griselda, edited by Donald Jay Grout.
9. The Operas of Alessandro Scarlatti, Donald Jay Grout, General Editor. Volume IV: The Faithful Princess, edited by Donald Jay Grout.
10. The Operas of Alessandro Scarlatti, Donald Jay Grout, General Editor. Volume V: Massimo Puppieno, edited by H. Colin Slim.
11. The Operas of Alessandro Scarlatti, Donald Jay Grout, General Editor. Volume VI: La caduta de' Decemviri, edited by Hermine Weigel Williams.
12. The Operas of Alessandro Scarlatti, Donald Jay Grout, General Editor. Volume VII: Gli equivoci nel sembiante, edited by Frank A. D'Accone.
13. The Operas of Alessandro Scarlatti, Donald Jay Grout, General Editor. Volume VIII: Tigrane, edited by Michael Collins.
14. The Instrumental Music of Giovanni Legrenzi. Sonate a due e tre, Opus 2. Edited by Stephen Bonta.
15. The Operas of Alessandro Scarlatti, Donald Jay Grout, General Editor. Volume IX: La Statira, edited by William C. Holmes.

Harvard Publications in Music, 15

THE OPERAS OF ALESSANDRO SCARLATTI

Donald Jay Grout, General Editor
with the assistance of Hermine Williams
Volume IX

THE OPERAS OF ALESSANDRO SCARLATTI

Volume IX

LA STATIRA

Edited by William C. Holmes

Harvard University Press
Cambridge, Massachusetts
and London, England

1985

Printed in the United States of America
10 9 8 7 6 5 4 3 2 1

This book is printed on acid-free paper, and its binding materials have been chosen for strength and durability.

Publication of this book has been aided by a grant from the L. J. Skaggs and Mary C. Skaggs Foundation.

Library of Congress Cataloging in Publication Data

Scarlatti, Alessandro, 1660–1725.
La Statira.
(The Operas of Alessandro Scarlatti; v. 9)
(Harvard publications in music; 15)
Libretto by Pietro Cardinal Ottoboni.
Based on: Moralia; Lives / Plutarch. Natural History / Pliny.
1. Operas—Scores. I. Holmes, William, 1928–
II. Ottoboni, Pietro, 1667–1740. III. Plutarch.
Moralia. IV. Plutarch. Vitae parallelae. V. Pliny,
the Elder. Naturalis historia. VI. Title. VII. Series:
Scarlatti, Alessandro, 1660–1725. Operas; v. 9.
VIII. Series; Harvard publications in music; 15.
M1500.S28S6 1984 83-26418
ISBN 0-674-64035-7

Acknowledgments

I wish, above all, to thank Donald J. Grout for his advice and his patience. Thanks are also in order to the University of California, Irvine, and to the American Council of Learned Societies for financial help. A special debt of gratitude is owed numerous friends and colleagues who have contributed their expertise on various matters: Edwin Hanley and Frank D'Accone from UCLA, Margaret Murata and H. Colin Slim from UC Irvine, Owen Jander from Wellesley College, and Lowell Lindgren from MIT. Robert A. Hall, Jr., and Franco Tonelli were generous with advice about translating seventeenth-century Italian.

Grateful acknowledgment is made especially to the Bayrische Staatsbibliothek, whose copy of the score is the basis for this edition. Other sources were also consulted from the Cardiff Public Library; the British Library; the Biblioteca Estense, Modena; the Conservatorio di San Pietro a Majella, Naples; the Bibliothèque du Conservatoire, Brussels; the Library of Congress, Washington, D.C.; and the Civico Museo Bibliografico Musicale, Bologna.

W.C.H.

Contents

Critical Notes are available from the Isham Memorial Library, Department of Music, Harvard University, Cambridge, Massachusetts, 02138.

INTRODUCTION

Pietro Cardinal Ottoboni, *La Statira*, and the Roman Carnival of 1690

The deaths of two prominent personages marked 1689 as an eventful year for the arts in Rome. The self-exiled Queen Christina of Sweden (1626–1689), who had been a leading figure in the Roman artistic world for more than thirty years, died on April 19, and with her death a brilliant era of private patronage came to an end. Less than four months later, on August 12, the death of Pope Innocent XI (Odescalchi, reg. 1676–1689) closed a pontificate that, although it had witnessed many political and diplomatic successes, had demonstrated little interest and even some hostility toward the world of the arts. Innocent was a reformer, and during his reign public secular entertainments of all kinds were kept at a minimum. In fact, Rome's largest public theater, the Tordinona, was closed for the length of his reign.[1] Soon after Innocent's death, the papacy and its attitudes toward the secular world changed drastically. By October 6, 1689, a conclave had elected a new pope, Pietro Ottoboni, who took the name of Alexander VIII (reg. 1689–1691). The Ottoboni were a wealthy, powerful Venetian family, and the new pope lost no time in showing the Romans that during his pontificate many of the secular glories of the earlier seventeenth century would be restored. He also quickly reverted to what had been known during the pontificate of Urban VIII (reg. 1623–1644) as the "Barberini disease": nepotism. Hardly had Alexander VIII ascended the papal throne than he called two of his nephews into his service. Marco became Castellano di S. Angelo, Generale delle Galere, and Duca di Fiano. Marco's brother, Antonio, became Principe di Soglio and Generale della Chiesa. Then, on November 7, 1689, Pietro Ottoboni, son of Antonio and great-nephew of the pope, was created Cardinal and Vice Cancelliere della Chiesa.

Young Pietruccio (1667–1740), as he was sometimes called to distinguish him from his great-uncle the pope, was the last and perhaps the most renowned member of his family. From the age of 22, when he became a cardinal, until his death he used his immense power and wealth to support the arts, especially music and the theater. For example, within six months after receiving his cardinal's hat the young Pietro had commissioned Alessandro Scarlatti to set a libretto which he had written and had added Arcangelo Corelli to the rolls of his household musicians.[2] The cardinal's residence at the palace of the Cancelleria, along with the Basilica of San Lorenzo adjacent to it, and the Tordinona theater soon became active centers for

1. The standard study on this theater and its history remains A. Cametti, *Il Teatro Tordinona poi di Apollo*, 2 vols. (Tivoli, 1938). For more on Innocent XI and his attitude toward the theater, see Frank A. D'Accone's Introduction to *Gli equivoci nel sembiante*, vol. VII of this series.
2. The basic study on Cardinal Ottoboni and music is H. J. Marx, "Die Musik am Hofe Pietro Ottobonis unter Arcangelo Corelli," in *Studien zur Italienisch-Deutschen Musikgeschichte* [*Analecta Musicologica*], V (Graz and Rome, 1968), 104–177. See also S. H. Hansell, "Orchestral Practice at the Court of Cardinal Pietro Ottoboni," in *Journal of the American Musicological Society*, XIX (Fall, 1966), 398–403.

some of the most splendid musical and theatrical performances held in seventeenth-century Rome.

Cardinal Ottoboni did not content himself with being merely a patron of the arts; he took an active part in them throughout his life. He fancied himself a poet of no mean accomplishment—a judgment, as we shall see, that was not always in agreement with that of contemporary critics. He was an active and illustrious member of the Arcadian Academy (under the pseudonym of Crateo Pradelini), and in addition to his support of the Tordinona theater, he built a private theater in the Cancelleria. During his lifetime Ottoboni wrote a number of poems and librettos for oratorios. Early in his career he also wrote five opera librettos, the second of which was *La Statira*.[3]

Late in 1689, the Tordinona theater was refurbished in preparation for the carnival season of 1690.[4] After having remained closed for more than fourteen years, the theater was in need of extensive redecoration, much of which was done at the personal expense of Cardinal Ottoboni. The new pope, the young cardinal, and indeed all of the Roman nobility were determined to make the carnival of 1690 one of the most lavish in decades. Their determination was rewarded with a carnival characterized by many brilliant receptions and other entertainments, as well as by a number of elaborate theatrical spectacles, both sung and spoken. These spectacles took place at the Tordinona, the Cancelleria, the Collegio Clementino, the Palazzo Rospigliosi, and the Palazzo Colonna, among other places. As it turned out, the carnival of 1690 was the only complete one to be witnessed by Alexander VIII. His death on February 1, 1691, abruptly cut short another equally brilliant season planned for that year. A pasquinade written soon after the pope's death ironically refers to his worldly predilections: "Great Pope, oh Pantalon, now dead, / Who loved his nephews more than sons, / Protected gondoliers and their songs, / The actor, the buffoon, and the castrato ."[5]

The reopening of the Tordinona with a performance of Alessandro Scarlatti's *La Statira* on Thursday, January 5, 1690, inaugurated the carnival season of that year.[6] Critical reaction to the performance was mixed. An agent from Florence found the plot too sombre for the opening of carnival. "Thursday evening there was a per-

3. Ottoboni's five opera librettos written before 1700 are *L'amante del suo nemico* (music by Flavio Carlo Lanciani, 1688), *La Statira, Amore et gratitudine* (music by Flavio Carlo Lanciani, 1690), *Il Colombo, ossia l'India scoperta* (composer unknown, 1690, performed in Rome, 1691), and *La forza dell'innocenza* (unfinished, 1690?).
4. In 1690 carnival began on January 5, the eve of Epiphany, Shrove Tuesday fell on February 7, Ash Wednesday on February 8, and Easter on March 26.
5. Rome, Biblioteca nazionale centrale [Rnaz], Fondo Vittorio Emmanuele, Cod. 302 [VE 302]. *Miscellanea di satire e pasquinate pubblicate in Roma durante le sedi vacanti di Clemente X, Innocenzo XI, ed Alessandro VIII, sui papi morti, sui conclavi, e su altre faccende politiche di quell'epoca*, #210, 133^{v}.

   Gran Papa, O Pantaloni, ora mancato
   Un ch'amò più i nipoti ch'i figlioli
   Protegge goldolieri e barcaroli,
   Il comico, il buffone, et il castrato.
6. A wealth of information concerning the performances of *La Statira* and other operas performed during the carnival season of 1690 has been preserved in the following documents:

   Florence, Archivio di Stato [*Fas*], Mediceo 3956. *Roma e Stato della Chiesa. Lettere Abatte Mancini.*
   Fas, Mediceo 3408. *Sig. Ab. Mancini, Lettere e minuti.*
   Modena, Archivio di Stato [*MOas*], Busta 67 [66]. *Avvisi di Roma.*
   MOas, Cavalleria Ducale-Estero. Ambasciatori, Agenti e correspondenti Estense, Italia, Roma, Vol. 259. *Carteggi dell'Abbate Panziroli.*
   Rome, Biblioteca Apostolica Vaticana [*Rvat*], Ottob. Lat. 3356. *Avvisi di Roma.*
   Rvat, Computisteria Ottoboni, Giustificazioni. Vol. 13 [1454]. Vol. 14 [1451]. Vol. 15 [1457]. Vol. 18 [1458]. Vol. 20 [1455].

formance, for the first time, at the Tordinona, of a work by Cardinal Ottoboni. It was successful because of its magnificent scenery and costumes, but was a melancholy work; there was a great crowd in attendance."[7] A correspondent from Modenz was equally unimpressed. "Thursday evening there was, for the first time, a performance at the Tordinona. It appears, generally, to have been applauded for its music, for the scenery, and for the singers, but not very much for the text. At the end of the performance Fame was to have descended on a machine singing the praises of the Ottoboni family; but Don Antonio [the cardinal's father] was opposed to the idea and wanted something else to be sung. His son decided not to use the machine."[8] Another correspondent from Modena was favorable to the entire production, but took pains especially to praise a singer who was in the service of the Duke of Modena. "Among the many operas heard here, the only successful one is that at the Tordinona, in which our own Sig. Borosini sings, and he is applauded as the best of all the singers. He also sings the principal role of Oronte."[9] Writing later, sometime after Alexander VIII's death, Pasquino added his critical opinion to those of greater minds. In a satire entitled "The Singers, Pimps, Whores [who] with all Vice triumph under the direction of Alexander VIII and [his] Nephews," which begins with the line, "Oh singers, your pope is now dead," he declares: "The bad poetry of your cardinal, / Expressed in *Statira* and *Colombo* / You sang there, it is true, but without high regard.[10]

The sources document other performances of *La Statira* at the Tordinona during carnival on January 11, January 24, and February 6. After this last performance on the Monday preceding Ash Wednesday Don Antonio Ottoboni used the Tordinona as a setting for a gala "festino" in Venetian style. According to contemporary accounts, the body of the theater itself was sumptuously decorated and an orchestra descended on a machine to provide music while the guests danced and dined upon elaborate food provided in their boxes.[11]

Lent followed and with it the closing of the theaters. During this period the sets of *La Statira* were moved to the Cancelleria. Two weeks after Easter, on April 9, *La Statira* was performed at the Cancelleria—but this performance was announced as an oratorio:[12] There were two further performances at the Cancelleria on April 16 and April 19, 1690.

This opera by Ottoboni and Scarlatti was apparently never performed again.

7. *Fas,* Mediceo 3956. Letter of January 7, 1690. "Giovedì sera si fece la comedia per la prima volta nel Teatro di Tor di Nona, opera del Sig. Cardinale Ottoboni che riuscì per scene, e abiti molto magnifica, ma parve malinconica assai, e vi fu un concorso grandissimo."

8. *MOas,* Busta 67 [66]. Letter of January 7, 1690. "Giovedì sera si fece per la prima volta la Comedia di Tor di Nona e pare che generalmente habbia applauso per la musica, per le scene e per i Musici, ma non gran cosa per le parole. In fine della detta comedia doveva venire in machina la Fama cantando lodi della Casa Ottoboni: ma Don Antonio si è opposto esortando a farli cantare qualche altra cosa, et il figlio ha voluto che non vi sia più la detta machina."

9. *MOas,* Cavalleria Ducale, Vol. 259. "Tra le altre opere che si sentono in musica ha solo il grido quella del teatro di Tordinona, nella quale recita il nostro sig. Borosini con applauso di essere il migliore cantante di tutti, havendo anco la prima parte ch'è l'*Oronte.*" The tenor Antonio Borosini (*ca.* 1660–?) spent time in the service of Francesco I at Modena, although he sang in many other places, principally Hannover and Vienna. See the biographical entry by C. Casellato in *Dizionario biografico degli italiani,* vol. 12, 806–807.

10. *Rnaz,* VE 302, #308, 146r.
Dal vostro cardinale la bassa rima
Nella Statira e nel Colombo espressa,
Cantaste è ver colà, ma senza stima.
On *Il Colombo,* see n. 3.

11. For a description of this "festino," see the *Mémoires* of the Marquis de Coulanges printed in A. Ademollo, *I teatri di Roma nel secolo decimosettimo* (Rome, 1888), 179–180. Further information can be found in *Fas,* Mediceo 3956 and 3408; *MOas Avvisi,* Busta 67 [66] and Cavalleria Ducale, vol. 259; and *Rvat, Comp. Ottob.,* vol. 13 [1454], fasc. 158, 184, and 226.

12. *Fas,* Mediceo 3956, letters of April 8 and 11. *Fas,* Mediceo 3408, letter of April 11.

There are no reports that it enjoyed revivals in other cities at other times as did many of Scarlatti's operas. Giazotto's listing of a performance at Genoa in 1710 (based on a printed catalogue of performances in that city published *ca.* 1772) is almost certainly unfounded. Neither composer nor librettist is mentioned in the catalogue, and no printed libretto bearing that date, 1710, is known to exist.[13] As will be seen below, a different *La Statira* is a better candidate for the Genoese performances. Ottoboni's libretto, much altered, was used for an opera performed at the Capranica theater at Rome in 1726, but for this production the music was composed by Tomaso Albinoni.[14]

Other bits of information about *La Statira* survive, among them the names of three of the singers who took part in the Roman performances: Pasqualino T(h)iepoli, Bartolomeo Monaci da Montalcino, and Antonio Borosini.[15] There also exists an itemized bill for all of the costume materials used at the performances in the Cancelleria, a bill which gives more than a hint of the enormous expenses incurred for the production and the sumptuousness of its presentation.[16]

Statira in History and in Dramatic Literature

Statira, the name of both the wife and the daughter of Darius, King of Persia, is discussed by Plutarch in his *Moralia*, Vol. IV, "On the Fortune or the Virtue of Alexander, II" and in his *Lives* , Vol. VII, "Alexander," Chapters LXX and LXXVII.[17] As recounted by Plutarch, in 333 B.C. after the battle of Issus, when Alexander defeated Darius, the family of Darius was captured, although Darius himself escaped and was killed sometime later. Plutarch lauds Alexander for his chivalrous treatment of the Persian women. Nine years later, after his return from India, Alexander married Statira, the daughter, at Susa. It was a political move, designed to unite the two peoples, and Alexander at the same time induced many of his officers to take Persian brides. The death of Statira, as described by Plutarch, was arranged by Roxanne, the favorite mistress of Alexander and mother of his son. Roxanne had Statira's body stuffed in a well, and the well filled with dirt.

During the seventeenth and early eighteenth centuries, Statira enjoyed considerable popularity as a dramatic protagonist. With the exceptions of Ottoboni's libretto and a French play, dramatists chose not to treat her story as it was reported by Plutarch.

The earliest libretto to be entitled *Statira* is that by Giovanni Francesco Busenello, with music by Cavalli, printed in 1655.[18] The work, as stated by Busenello in his preface, was his first since that of *L'incoronazione di Poppea* written some thirteen

13. R. Giazotto, *La musica a Genova* (Genoa, 1941), 200–202 and 329. Recently, documents have been found that would seem to indicate that parts of Scarlatti's *La Statira* were performed, without costumes, in Rome on February 10, 1706. See Thomas Edward Griffin, "The Late Baroque Serenata in Rome and Naples: A Documentary Study with Emphasis on Alessandro Scarlatti" (unpublished dissertation, University of California, Los Angeles, 1983), 495–496.
14. Cametti, *Teatro Tordinona,* 345. O. G. T. Sonneck incorrectly states that his libretto was by Zeno and Pariati. See his *Catalogue of Opera Librettos Published before 1800* (Washington, D.C., 1914), 1034.
15. On Borosini, see n. 9. On Montalcino and Thiepoli, see Marx, note 2 above, 173 and 176. On published broadsides dedicated to characters in *La Statira,* see L. Lindgren and C. Schmidt, "A Collection of 137 Broadsides Concerning Theatre in Late Seventeenth-Century Italy: An Annotated Catalogue," in *Harvard Library Bulletin*, vol. XXVIII, no. 2 (April 1980), 207.
16. *Rvat, Comp. Ottob.* vol. 15 [1457], fasc. 648.
17. Loeb Classical Library edition, IV, 451, and VII, 419, 437.
18. Venice, Biblioteca nazionale di San Marco [*Vnm*], Dramm. 1140.1. La Statira/ Principessa/ di Persia/ Drama/ Per Musica/ . . . / di Gio. Francesco Busenello/ . . . / in Venetia, MDLV.

years earlier. Ottoboni's libretto is the next known setting of the story. Following this, a French tragedy, *La Statira*, by Nicolas Pradon appeared in 1695.[19] In this five-act version which roughly follows Plutarch, Statira and Roxanne are rivals and Roxanne has Statira murdered. The copy of Pradon's tragedy in the Biblioteca Marciana at Venice is from the personal library of Apostolo Zeno. Zeno himself in 1705 collaborated with Pietro Pariati on a *Statira*, set to music by Francesco Gasparini.[20] Although Zeno knew the play by Pradon and presumably had some knowledge of Plutarch, this *Statira* has no dramatic connection with either. As stated earlier, Ottoboni's libretto served as the basis of a Roman production of *La Statira*, set by Tomaso Albinoni in 1726. Ottoboni's name is not mentioned in the libretto, but Valesio's *Diario* attributes it to him, adding that the libretto was "very much changed."[21] In 1741, Carlo Goldoni wrote a *Statira* libretto, set by Pietro Chiarini,[22] and in 1742, Francesco Silvani's *La Statira*, with music by Nicola Porpora, appeared.[23]

Ottoboni's libretto incorporates elements from Plutarch, and adds the story of the painter Apelles as reported by Pliny in his *Natural History*, Book XXXV, Chapter 36 (both the autograph libretto and the printed libretto incorrectly say Chapter 10.)[24] The common bonds between these stories are the life and activities of Alexander the Great. From Plutarch come those parts dealing with the battle between Alexander and Darius, with the death of Darius, the capture of Statira, and Alexander's humane treatment of her and the other Persian prisoners of war. From Pliny, Ottoboni extracted the tale of Apelles, who painted the portrait of Alexander's mistress Pancaspe (called "Campaspe" in the libretto). After having finished the portrait, Apelles fell in love with Pancaspe, whereupon Alexander magnanimously presented her to the painter. Ignoring historical and chronological accuracy, Ottoboni successfully combined these two plotlines to make a dramatically compact libretto with strong character delineations.

Specifically, Ottoboni's plot revolves around a number of events and intrigues which take place after the defeat of the Persian army by Alexander. Darius is dead and his daughter, Statira, is taken captive by the Macedonians. Statira, who is betrothed to the Persian prince Orontes, becomes the object of Alexander's affections. However, Alexander is loved by Campaspe, who in turn is loved from afar by the court painter, Apelles, and the Macedonian general, Demetrius. The jealous Campaspe conspires, unsuccessfully, to have Statira murdered, enlisting the unwilling aid of Demetrius. After many further complications the fabled magnanimity of Alexander provides a happy dénouement—but with a twist. Apelles and Campaspe, who during the course of the opera come to love one another, are united. Alexander reunites Statira and Orontes, at the same time renouncing his throne and empire in favor of Statira because of his love for her. Orontes' honor, however, cannot allow such a sacrifice on Alexander's part; thus Orontes withdraws, Statira accepts Alexander's offer of marriage, and all ends happily for the two principal pairs of characters.

19. *Vnm,* Dramm. 3592.5. *Le/ Théâtre/ de/ Mr./ DE PRADON* . . / A PARIS/ Chez la Veuve Mabre Cramoist/ M.DC.XCV.
20. *Vnm,* Dramm. 1198.1. Statira/ Drama per Musica/ . . / In Venezia, M.DCCV/ Appresso Marino Rossetti. Perhaps this was the *Statira* performed at Genoa in 1710.
21. The entry for February 18, 1726, states that the opera "composta dal Cardinale Ottoboni e recitata per la prima volta nel teatro di T.[ordinona] l'anno 1690 ed ora assai riformata" did not enjoy success. See Cametti, *Teatro Tordinona*, 345. See also n. 13.
22. *Vnm,* Dramm. 1253.3. Statira/ Dramma/ Per Musica/ Del Dr. C.G./ . . / l'anno 1741/ . . . in Venetia/ Per Marino Rossetti.
23. *Vnm,* Dramm. 1058. STATIRA/ Dramma per Musica/ . . . / 1742.
24. Loeb Classical Library edition, IX, 325.

Sources

Only major differences among the sources will be noted in the following descriptions. All other variants, textual and musical, can be found in the Critical Notes. In the lists of sources given here, italicized sigla are those used by the editor both in the text and in the Critical Notes. Following each of these, the location of the source is indicated by the standard sigla used in the *Répertoire International des Sources Musicales* (RISM).

Librettos:	*Rvat*	I: Rvat	Ms. Ottoboni Lat. 2360
	Rom	I: Bc	
Scores:	*Bc*	B: Bc	Ms. 2348-k
	Dlb	D: Dlb	
	Wc	US: Wc	M 1500 S28 S6
	Mbs	D: Mbs	Mus. Ms. 144
	CDp	GB: CDp	Mackworth Collection
	MOe	I: MOe	Ms. F. 1538
	Lbm	GB: Lbm	Ms. add. 22.103

Librettos

Rvat: Biblioteca Apostolica Vaticana, Ottoboni Lat. 2360. Quite unusually for works of this period, there exists an autography libretto of *La Statira*. It is found in a manuscript volume that appears to be a workbook, for it contains texts of other librettos by Ottoboni, plot synopses, and literary annotations of various kinds. *La Statira* opens the volume, and ends on f. 37^{v} where Ottoboni wrote "fine del dramma li 4 Marzo 1689." The manuscript carries a number of revisions—cuts, substitutions, and the like—but the opera as set in the scores can, with few exceptions, be found here.

Rom: Bologna, Civico Museo Bîbliografico Musicale.[25] There is only one printed edition of the libretto of *La Statira*, that issued by Giovanni Francesco Buagni at Rome in 1690. The title page reads

> *LA STATIRA* / Dramma / per Musica / Recitato nel Teatro di / Torre di Nona. / L'Anno 1690. / Dedicato / ALLE DAME / di Roma. / Emblem] / In Roma, Per Gio: Francesco Buagni 1690. / Con licenza de' Superiori. Sivendono in bottega di Francesco Leone / Libraro in Piazza Madama.

There are sixty-eight pages, followed by three unnumbered pages of textual additions. Preceding p. 1, there is a view of St. Mark's square, from the Bacino, over which hovers a large angel playing a trumpet and holding a banner on which appear the arms of the Ottoboni family. On p. 2 is the imprimatur, followed on p. 3 by the dedication "To the Ladies of Rome," signed by Francesco Leone. Then follow the *Argomento* (p. 5), the cast of characters and descriptions of the dances (p. 7), and the changes of scene in each act (p. 8). Neither the librettist nor the composer is mentioned.

The unnumbered pages of textual additions at the end contain texts for Nos. 82, 83, 85, and 86 (Act III, sc. 5, wrongly labeled Act II, sc. 5), and for Nos. 113, 114, and 115 (the speeches of the goddess Diana in Act III, sc. 16, the final scene of the opera.)

A comparison of the printed libretto with the autograph libretto reveals many significant differences. These differences are discussed at length elsewhere.[26] For

25. For a list of other libraries owning copies of the printed libretto, see G. Rostirolla's catalogue in R. Pagano and L. Bianchi, *Alessandro Scarlatti* (Turin, 1972), 339.
26. For descriptions of *Rom* and *Rvat*, as well as a detailed comparison of the textual sources and transcriptions of the documents connected with the performances of Ottoboni's *La Statira*, see my *La Statira by Pietro Ottoboni and Alessandro Scarlatti: The Textual Sources, With a Documentary Postscript* (New York, 1983).

present purposes, it will suffice to mention only those important ones which affect the musical setting of the work as we know it. The autograph libretto contains a prologue with the allegorical figures of Tempo and Fortuna and the goddess Pallade as its characters. This prologue is not present either in the printed libretto or in the scores, although Ottoboni apparently considered it to be an integral part of the opera. Two of its characters appear in the original, discarded title of the opera—*Virtù, Tempo, e Fortuna*—and are referred to, by various literary conceits, many times in the version of the opera that was set by Scarlatti. The added texts in the printed libretto for Nos. 82, 83, 85, and 86 are set in all the musical sources, but are lacking in the autograph. Likewise, the added texts in the printed libretto for Nos. 113, 114, and 115, set in all the scores except *Lbm*, are lacking in the autograph libretto. No. 9, which appears in *Rom* as Act I, sc. 3, and is set in all the scores, is also lacking from autograph libretto. These additions provide ample evidence that many changes were made after the body of the libretto was printed.

Scores

Bc: Brussels, Bibliothèque du Conservatoire, Ms. 2348-k.

Dlb: Dresden, DDR, Sächsische Landesbibliothek.

Wc: Washington, D.C., Library of Congress, M 1500 S28 S6.

Bc and *Dlb* are modern copies of *Mbs*, and *Wc* is a modern copy of *Lbm*; thus these scores have not been used in the preparation of this edition.

With few exceptions, all of the contemporary, or nearly contemporary, surviving scores (*Mbs*, *Lbm*, *CDp*, and *MOe*) present versions of the opera that agree with one another quite remarkably.

Mbs: Munich, Bayrische Staatsbibliothek, Mus. Ms. 144. This is a sumptuous volume in oblong format, bound in red leather with decorative gold stamping. On both the front and the back of the binding appears the coat of arms of the Ottoboni family. The manuscript was acquired from the Bibliothek Hauser in 1828. It is this manuscript that was used by Lorenz in his discussion of the opera.[27] In 1977 the manuscript was provided with a new foliation that differs from the editorial pagination used in the Critical Notes for his edition. Thus, in the Critical Notes, page 1 of *Mbs* corresponds to f. 3^r of the new foliation in the manuscript, and the last page of music, p. 686, corresponds to f. 346^v in the manuscript.

Entries in the household accounts of Cardinal Ottoboni indicate that this manuscript was probably copied by Tarquinio Lanciani, the supposed brother of the better-known Flavio Carlo Lanciani (1661–1706), who was also in the service of Ottoboni.[28] Tarquinio's birth and death dates are unknown, but he was on the Ottoboni household's payrolls from 1691 to 1693. Even before he became attached officially to Ottoboni's retinue, Tarquinio had copied music for the cardinal. *Mbs* has no title page. On an otherwise blank page at the beginning is written, "Del cavaliere Scarlatti: scritta p[er] il musico Appianisci." The score lacks a sinfonia, and begins directly with Act I, sc. 1.

CDp: Cardiff, Cardiff Public Library, Mackworth Collection. This score is in three volumes, one for each act of the opera. It is in oblong format and copied in a late-seventeenth-century hand. There is no sinfonia. Within the large ornamental

27. A. Lorenz, *Alessandro Scarlattis Jugendoper*, 2 vols. (Augsburg, 1927); vol. 1, 119–130; vol. 2, 111–130.

28. The supposed brothers Tarquinio and Carlo Flavio Lanciani pose as yet unsolved biographical and bibliographical questions in any study of Cardinal Ottoboni's musical establishment. Some information about them is summarized in Marx, note 2 above, 171. The birth and death dates of Carlo Flavio given by Marx, and in *The New grove*, 1665–1724, have been corrected by Giorgio Morelli to 1661–14 July 1706 in his "Giovanni Andrea Lorenzani artista e letterato romano del seicento," in *Studi secenteschi*, vol. XIII (1972), 198 Flavio Carlo Lanciani looms large in the creation of the final musical version of *La Statira*, as will be seen later.

capital N[otte] at the head of Act I, sc. 1, is written, "La Statira del sig. Aless.º Scarlatti."

MOe: Modena, Biblioteca Estense, Ms. F. 1538. This score is in oblong format, copied in a late-seventeenth-century hand. In this manuscript, unlike the others in most cases, the vocal part is often, but not always, copied directly above the bass line and below the other instrumental parts. On the spine of *MOe* is written ORONTE which has been crossed out. It is interesting that the Este manuscript should have had this title because Antonio Borosini, an Este singer, sang the role of Oronte in the first performances of *La Statira*. *MOe*, then, may have been Borosini's personal copy of the score. On the title page, in a nineteenth-century hand, is written, "La Statira Autore incerto/ Atti 3, con istromenti." There is a sinfonia before which appears the inscription, "Sinfonia avanti l'alzar della tenda."

Lbm: London, The British Library, Ms. add. 22.103. This volume, in a late-seventeenth-century hand, is in oblong format. The title page reads *La Statira/Poesia del em:mo Cardinale Ottoboni/ Musica del Sig:r Aless:o Scarlatti*. On the following page is written, "Purchase of C. Hamilton/ 12 Sept. 1857." There is a sinfonia with many copyist's errors, most notably the complete miscopying of mm. 53–61, which make no musical sense whatsoever. The music for Diana in Act III, sc. 16, is lacking. As stated above, this text formed part of the texts appended at the end of the printed libretto.

The lack of Diana's text and music in *Lbm* is one instance of substantial disagreement among the musical sources. Because Diana's text appears at the end of the printed libretto, one might suppose that *Lbm* stems from a version of the opera that more closely resembles the "original" one as it appears in the body of the printed libretto. This, however, is not the case for *Lbm* sets the other added texts, from Act III, sc. 5, that are printed with those of Diana.[29] One might also suppose that economic factors determined the deletion of Diana's scene. Her appearance requires another soprano in the cast because all of the opera's characters are on stage when she enters. This explanation is not convincing for the documents state that no expense was spared for the production of *La Statira* at the Tordinona. A more likely possibility is that *Lbm* presents the opera as it was performed at the private theater in the Cancelleria, after Easter, in 1690. It is known that the theater was small and could not have been equipped with the machinery necessary for Diana's appearance. The entrance of the goddess has nothing to do with the drama, and we know that it was added solely to make use of the machines in the large theater. Cutting it from a performance would subtract nothing from the dénouement.

Another instance of substantial disagreement among sources, though of a different sort, occurs in Act II, sc. 7. Here, the scores agree among themselves but disagree with both the autograph and printed librettos. The librettos present the text of this scene in an order that differs considerably from the arrangement of the text in all of the musical sources. The order of the Numbers as they appear in the libretto is as follows:

No. 54
No. 55, to. m. 10
No. 52
No. 53
No. 55, from m. 10
No. 56
No. 57
No. 58

CDp and *MOe* divide this one scene into two parts and give Nos. 52 and 53 as sc. 7 and Nos. 54–58 as sc. 8. An extensive scenic description appears in *CDp* and *MOe* at

29. See the description of *Rom* for details.

the beginning of their sc. 8 (No. 54). In *Rvat* and in this edition—but not in *Rom*, which has no scenic description—this long rubric appears at the beginning of sc. 7 (No. 52). It is not clear why the arrangement of the text is as it is in the musical sources, nor why the scenic description appears where it does in *CDp* and *MOe*. The arrangement of the text in the libretto is more logical and makes more dramatic sense. Furthermore, the copyist of *Mbs* apparently became confused at the point in No. 55 (between mm. 9 and 10) where the text had been altered. He began to copy the opening speech of No. 52, that is, the text as it appears in the libretto, then realized there had been a change. He crossed out a measure, forgot to complete the cadence of Campaspe's preceding recitative, and continued copying the new, altered version.

There are a number of manuscript collections of arias containing selections from *La Statira*.[30] Of these, three deserve special mention because they raise certain questions, not all of which can be answered at present. Because of their fundamental importance, I shall give summary descriptions of the three manuscripts here, and present their problematic aspects.

The largest collection of arias is at Naples, Conservatorio di San Pietro a Majella, M. 34.5.13. This volume, which was copied in 1693, opens with an *Aria con eco di quattro violini* ("Antri voi d'un core amante") and closes with a cantata, *Il Leandro* ("Su le sponde d'Abbido"). Both of these works carry attributions to Scarlatti. The central portion of the manuscript consists of settings of either one or both stanzas of twenty-eight arias from *La Statira*, the vast majority of which agree both textually and musically with the printed libretto and the scores. There are important exceptions to this. Three arias have texts that do not appear in any of the musical sources of the opera as we know it. Surprisingly, these very texts appear in the autograph libretto as parts of scenes that were completely cut from the final version of the opera ("Quanto dolce di chi s'ama," "Mi fidai della speranza," and "Fosco nembo in giorno estivo"). Furthermore, the Naples collection contains four settings of stanzas that appear only in the autograph libretto ("S'ella è vaga," the first stanza of No. 53; "Offeso mio core," "Se quel sol l'amato oggetto," and "Dei tuoi sospiri," the second stanzas of Nos. 62, 99, and 102 respectively). Finally, and to further cloud the already murky waters, there are two texts in the Naples collection that appear both in the printed libretto and the scores but that are here set to different music ("Chi a volo troppo alto," No. 58, and "Cor avvezzo," No. 109).[31]

Two other manuscript collections of arias are of interest for quite different reasons. Chigi Q.IV.37, at the Vatican Library, and Rés. Vmf. ms. 40, at the Bibliothèque Nationale in Paris, both raise the issue of musical attribution.[32] The Chigi collection is a sloppily assembled patchwork of 12 arias copied in at least two hands. Eight of these arias are attributed to Flavio Carlo Lanciani, and six of these eight, all copied in the same hand, are from *La Statira*:

"Chi a volo troppo alto," No. 58
"Dolce invidia," No. 115
"Tiranno, e che pretendi," No. 70
"Crudo cielo, empio fato," No. 9
"La clemenza nel cor," No. 29
"Viva pur l'arco," No. 113.

The Paris collection contains, among other pieces, six settings of texts from *La Statira*. Five of these (Nos. 25, 19, 33, 3, and 47) are attributed to Scarlatti. The sixth, however, is attributed to Flavio Carlo Lanciani: "Esser potrai crudele," (No. 43).

30. See Rostirolla's catalogue entry in Pagano and Bianchi, *Scarlatti*, 339–340.
31. The musical settings of Nos. 58 and 109, as they appear in the Naples collection, are printed in the Appendix.
32. I should like to thank Lowell E. Lindgren for drawing these manuscripts to my attention. Neither manuscript is mentioned in Rostirolla's catalogue.

The existence of these manuscripts and the information they contain raise two basic questions: why does the Naples collection have settings of texts that appear only in the autograph libretto? And why do the Chigi and Paris collections attribute the musical settings of some arias from *La Statira* to another composer, in this case Flavio Carlo Lanciani? The following observations may provide some answers.[33]

It seems logical to assume that all of the music in the Naples collection was composed by Scarlatti. The physical layout of the manuscript certainly supports this assumption; it opens and closes with works by Scarlatti. Between these two pieces are the twenty-eight settings of arias from *La Statira*. The music of the majority of these arias agrees with the extant scores. What then of those texts in the Naples collection that appear only in the autograph libretto? It is possible that at some time Scarlatti composed them, and that later the libretto was revised and certain scenes with their music were discarded. The copyist of the Naples collection, dated 1693, might well have had an earlier version of *La Statira* at hand. The different musical settings of "Chi a volo troppo alto" (No. 58) and "Cor avvezzo" (No. 109) are not so easily explained although they perhaps have some connection with the second question, to be discussed below.

Here, it will be useful to establish certain points in the chronology of events leading to the first performance of *La Statira*. Ottoboni finished his libretto at Rome in early March 1689, when Scarlatti was in Naples. He was probably in no hurry to have the libretto set to music because Innocent XI was still alive and Rome's theaters were still closed. To be sure, Ottoboni may have envisioned a private performance and could have sent a copy of the libretto to Scarlatti. In any case, Scarlatti left Naples and was in Rome from June through August 1689. It is also possible that Ottoboni and Scarlatti discussed the libretto during that period, although there is no known documentary evidence to support this possibility. Scarlatti was back in Naples by September, and there is no record of his having returned to Rome before the first performance of *La Statira* on January 5, 1690.

If Scarlatti composed an "original" version of the opera, one that utilized texts from the autograph libretto that have come down to us in the Naples collection, he probably would have done so during the late summer or early fall, that is, after his return to Naples and after the death of Innocent XI on August 12. When Ottoboni's great-uncle was elected pope on October 6, the way was then cleared for the reopening of the Tordinona theater and public performances of opera. Perhaps it was around this time that Ottoboni decided to make certain revisions that cut some of the music already composed by Scarlatti, and decided to have *La Statira* mounted as the first opera of the approaching carnival season.

As has always been the case with newly composed operas, the once-revised *La Statira* was subjected to further revisions, this time much closer to the date of the first performance. Some of these revisions appear in the body of the printed libretto, executed perhaps in late December 1689, while, even later, others were printed and appended at the end on extra pages. The most obvious example of last-minute revisions is Diana's appearance on a cloud in Act III, sc. 16, the final scene of the opera. The documents tell that, originally, the allegorical figure of Fame was to have appeared singing in praise of the Ottoboni family. Cardinal Ottoboni's father, Don Antonio, forbade the use of this scene.[34] Diana's appearance was the evident compromise, and Diana's text accordingly is among those printed at the very end of the libretto.

Because of the press of time, it seems logical to suppose that Ottoboni would call in a composer resident in Rome to set the last-minute revisions to music. It is also logical to assume that he would engage one whom he knew and respected.

33. For a detailed discussion of these questions, see my *La Statira by Pietro Ottoboni and Alessandro Scarlatti.*

34. Ibid. and n. 8 for the documents.

Flavio Carlo Lanciani was an obvious candidate. He had been a member of Ottoboni's household since 1688, along with Corelli and a number of famous singers, and had earlier set another libretto by Ottoboni, *L'amante del suo nemico* (Rome, 1688). Music closer chronologically to *La Statira* is Lanciani's setting of Ottoboni's pastorale *Amore et gratitudine*, performed a number of times during the fall of 1690, little more than six months after the final performances of *La Statira*. Given the close economic and artistic connections between the cardinal and the composer, it is not difficult to accept Lanciani as the composer of those arias attributed to him in the Chigi and Paris collections.

Of the six arias attributed to Lanciani in the Chigi collection, five are not in the autograph libretto but appear in the printed libretto: Nos. 9, 29, and 70 in the body of the libretto and Nos. 113 and 115 among the texts printed at the end. The text of the sixth aria, "Chi a volo troppo alto" (No. 58), appears in both the autograph and in the printed libretto. The music, attributed to Lanciani in the Chigi collection, is the same as that found in all of the complete scores of the opera. As mentioned earlier, "Chi a volo troppo alto" has different music in the Naples collection. I mention here parenthetically that precisely the same situation applies to "Cor avvezzo" (No. 109), the only other aria from the opera that survives in two versions. In the case of "Cor avvezzo" however, there is no extant attribution of the aria to Lanciani. At present it is not possible to ascertain why Lanciani might have recomposed arias already set by Scarlatti (assuming that the settings in the Naples collection are by Scarlatti). Perhaps it was done at the request of the singers.

Not all of the texts unique to the printed libretto are in the Chigi collection. This is not surprising when one recalls that the Chigi volume is a patchwork collection of arias copied by different hands. In all probability, portions of earlier manuscripts were lost before they were assembled and bound together in this volume. Thus, the six arias attributed to Lanciani, all copied by the same person, perhaps represent only part of his contribution to the final version of the score. For example, the settings of the added text in Act III, sc. 5 (Nos. 82, 83, and 85) might well be by Lanciani.

Finally, a word about "Esser portrai crudele" (No. 43), attributed to Lanciani in the Paris collection. The text setting of this aria is garbled in all of the musical scores of the opera.[35] It is difficult to explain why this is so, but there might be some connection between the garbled settings and the fact that "Esser potrai crudele" is the sole instance in the opera where a text from the autograph libretto is replaced by another text in the printed libretto with absolutely no indication for such a substitution by Ottoboni in the autograph. It is equally intriguing, and equally inexplicable, that the texting of "Esser potrai crudele" in the Paris collection is the only musical source to follow the ordering of the text in the printed libretto exactly.

Editorial Practice

The editorial procedures followed in this series have been discussed in the preceding volumes. Suffice it here to mention only those that have a specific connection with *La Statira*. Complete information on all editorial matters can be found in the Critical Notes, which are available from the Isham Memorial Library, Music Department, Harvard University.

1. In the surviving scores all arias are fully copied out. In this edition, the indications Da Capo and Dal Segno have been used whenever possible. This has been feasible because only on very rare occasions are there differences between the A sections in an ABA aria.

35. See the Critical Notes for details.

2. The notation of accidentals within a measure has been brought into line with modern practice.

3. In this edition all tempo marks, dynamic marks, figures in the basso continuo, and "solo" and "tutti" indications are conflations. If any of these appears in any one of the sources, it appears here also—except in the few cases of obvious mistakes. Any editorial additions appear in italics.

4. The stage directions in most cases are those from the printed libretto. Any not appearing in the translation of the libretto have been taken from one of the scores.

5. Because *La Statira* stems from the earlier part of Scarlatti's career, there are fewer notational problems than in his scores from a later period. In only one aria, No. 54, has it been necessary to alter the basic notation. All of the scores except CDp make use of a notational convention found in many seventeenth-century scores: black notes to denote hemiola. Thus, in measures corresponding to mm. 12–13, 20–21, 24–25, etc., the black notation,

has been changed to conform with CDp and modern usage,

6. All key signatures, both in the arias and in one recitative (No. 94), have been left as they appear in the sources.

7. In Act II there are considerable differences in scene numbering among the sources. This edition follows the scene numbering as it appears in *Rom*.

Performance Notes

The Orchestra

Although not all arias carry exact indications all the time, it is clear from the sources that the orchestra for *La Statira* consists of two violins, viola (sometimes called "violetta"), and basso continuo. In two Numbers only is this orchestra augmented by other instruments: in No. 5 there is a solo obbligato trumpet and in No. 8 a "sinfonia di trombe," with two trumpets added to the string orchestra.

Fortunately, there is some documentation which gives us a good idea of the size of the orchestra used at Ottoboni's palace and at the Tordinona theater during the 1690s. Ottoboni's *Amore et gratitudine*, music by Flavio Lanciani, was performed at the Cancelleria in the fall of 1690 and at the Tordinona in January 1691. Surviving records of payments show that the orchestra consisted of four violins, two violas, one violoncello, one contrabass viol, and one keyboard instrument. Two trumpets were added for the prologue. On two occasions the orchestra was enlarged to include nineteen violins, six violas, eight violoncellos, and five contrabass viols, but this larger ensemble performed only the sinfonia at the beginning of the work. In both cases, the number of violins was balanced by the number of lower strings.[36] These figures, and especially the ratio between upper and lower strings, should serve as an accurate guide for present-day performances. Although one or two harpsichords, along with appropriate doubling of the bass line by a string instrument, might serve perfectly well for the basso continuo, it is probable that other instruments such as lute and theorbo would make welcome additions to the continuo group. For example, Mbs, CDp, and MOe have the rubric "senza cembalo" at

36. See Hansell, note 2 above, 401.

the beginning of No. 2, an accompanied recitative, yet all scores carry figures in the bass line. Surely, somebody other than the keyboard player filled in the harmonies.

In many Numbers there are explicit directions for the use of a solo string ("solo") as opposed to the full string section ("tutti"). Nos. 25 and 29 carry the rubric "due violini soli." Since both of these arias are scored for violins and basso continuo, this rubric should be read as "first and second violins only," that is, without a viola part, and not as "two solo violins."

Ornamentation in Recitatives and Arias

The use of appoggiaturas at cadences in recitatives and at times in the melodic lines of the arias has been discussed in detail in earlier volumes of this series. The same general practices apply to *La Statira*. However, as regards extensive ornamentation of the melodic line and the insertion of cadenzas, a word of caution is in order. *La Statira* must be performed in the late seventeenth-century tradition. This means, generally, that there is not a great deal of melodic ornamentation. Highly ornamented vocal lines became the rule only in the early eighteenth century. In addition, there are no instances of fermatas denoting the addition of an improvised cadenza in any of the sources. An example of very discreet use of melodic ornamentation can be found in No. 79 by comparing the beginnings of the first and second stanzas.

Over-dotting

This practice was never as widespread in Italy as it was in France. In *La Statira* there are only four Numbers in which this convention might be applied: Nos. 54, 93, 99, and the opening of the ritornello in No. 79. For the sake of rhythmic consistency between voice and instruments and within the instrumental body itself, in this ritornello it would seem the case to over-dot those notes and rests that do not have dots as well as those where dots appear.

Synopsis of the Plot

ACT I

Sc. 1 (Nos. 2–4). In the Persian camp, Prince Oronte reflects upon his love for Statira, but is interrupted by the sounds of battle.

Sc. 2 (Nos. 5–8). As the Macedonians engage the Persians in battle, Alessandro urges on his troops. It is understood that, during the battle, Dario is killed, his daughter Statira taken prisoner, and the Persian army defeated.

Sc. 3 (No. 9). Oronte, alone, bemoans his fate, the death of Dario, and the loss of Statira.

Sc. 4 (Nos. 10–12). Dario's body is laid out in his tent. Statira mourns his death and wishes for her own.

Sc. 5 (Nos. 13–17). General Demetrio of the Macedonians and the servant Perinto came upon Statira. She asks that her father's body be given a decent burial. Demetrio consents, and also releases her from her bonds.

Sc. 6 (Nos. 18, 19). Campaspe, Alessandro's favorite, awaits his return from battle and muses on their love.

Sc. 7 (Nos. 20, 21). Apelle, Alessandro's court painter who is secretly in love with Campaspe, and Oronte, disguised as an Armenian, enter. Apelle lets it be known that Alessandro has become taken with Statira. This revelation produces various reactions: Campaspe is furious and jealous, Oronte is unhappy, and Apelle hopes that he might now press his suit with Campaspe.

Sc. 8 (Nos. 22, 23). Apelle and Oronte are left alone. Oronte promises great rewards to Apelle if Apelle can arrange for him to see Statira. Oronte leaves.

Sc. 9 (Nos. 24, 25). Alone, Apelle wonders if Campaspe will ever be his.

Sc. 10 (Nos. 26, 27). In a prison cell, Dario's body lies on a catafalque. Statira laments his death and invokes vengeance from the gods.

Sc. 11 (Nos. 28–31). Alessandro, Demetrio, and Perinto enter. Statira asks that Dario be buried and that she may be allowed to live out her days alone in a remote place. Alessandro tries to dissuade her, but finally consents to her wishes. Statira expresses her gratitude.

Sc. 12 (Nos. 32, 33). Demetrio and Perinto try to persuade Alessandro to take Statira as his wife, but he tells them that he intends to accede to her request. Demetrio and Perinto leave, and Alessandro muses upon his mixed feelings toward love in general and Statira in particular.

Sc. 13 (Nos. 34, 35). In a courtyard, Demetrio confesses to Perinto that he himself loves Campaspe. Perinto suggests that they disguise the Armenian (Oronte) as a shepherd, send him to Statira's hut, and have him convince Statira to marry Alessandro. In this way, Campaspe would be free to marry another.

Sc. 14 (Nos. 36, 37). Perinto exhorts the Persian soldiers who have been set free to be happy.

ACT II

Sc. 1 (Nos. 38, 39). In a picture gallery containing portraits of both Campaspe and Statira, Alessandro and Apelle discuss the two women. Alessandro decides that Statira will be his wife and queen. He then tells Apelle that Campaspe shall be his.

Sc. 2 (Nos. 40–43). Campaspe enters and chides Alessandro for not having come to visit her upon his return from battle. He answers vaguely, and her previous jealous suspicions are confirmed. Apelle leaves.

Sc. 3 (Nos. 44, 45). Statira enters, thanks Alessandro for releasing her soldiers, and again asks that she be allowed to retire in solitude immediately. Alessandro tries to dissuade her, she is adamant, and Campaspe is consumed with jealousy. Finally, Alessandro, once again, accedes to Statira's wishes. Alessandro leaves.

Sc. 4 (Nos. 46, 47). Statira thanks Campaspe for her kindnesses. Campaspe notes that Alessandro always kept her portrait with him, but that now there is also a portrait of Statira. Campaspe reflects upon the inconstancy of all lovers.

Sc. 5 (Nos. 48, 49). Oronte, disguised, enters and makes himself known to Statira. She asks him to remove her portrait. He then recounts his adventures: disguised as an Armenian, he was helped by Apelle, who in turn asked him to plead with Statira not to marry Alessandro. Apelle, because of his great love for Campaspe, and knowing that she wants to be Alessandro's wife, will do anything for her. Oronte agrees to take the portrait and Statira says that she will await him in her hut. She leaves.

Sc. 6 (Nos. 50, 51). Oronte, alone, reflects upon his love for Statira and upon the kindnesses of Apelle.

Sc. 7 (Nos. 52–58). Apelle, Alessandro, and Campaspe meet and discuss the situation. Alessandro will not have her and offers her to Apelle. She will not hear of this, and Alessandro reminds her that Icarus, too, set his sights too high. Alessandro leaves.

Sc. 8 (Nos. 59, 60). Campaspe is furious with Apelle and orders him to be off at once. He is heartbroken and bemoans his misfortune. Apelle leaves.

Sc. 9 (Nos. 61, 62). Demetrio and Perinto enter. Demetrio, because of his love for Campaspe, will do anything for her. She tells him that both Statira and Apelle must die. Then, and only then, will she consider his suit. He agrees. Campaspe leaves.

Sc. 10 (Nos. 63, 64). Perinto has reservations about the intended murders, but Demetrio resolves to carry them out.

Sc. 11 (Nos. 65–68). Statira, alone at Dario's mausoleum, still mourns her father. Exhausted from her sorrow, she falls asleep.

Sc. 12 (No. 69). Demetrio enters and hears Statira talking in her sleep. As he is about to murder her, a terrible storm and earthquake burst forth. Frightened, he flees.

ACT III

Sc. 1 (Nos. 70–72). Alessandro, alone, decries his confused state of mind. He finds he can still make no absolute decision between Campaspe and Statira.

Sc. 2 (Nos. 73, 74). Apelle, alone, is desolate that Campaspe has scorned him. He is about to commit suicide when Oronte appears.

Sc. 3 (No. 75). Oronte halts Apelle's suicide attempt. As they are arguing, they hear a woman's voice calling for help.

Sc. 4 (Nos. 76–79). Campaspe rushes in, pursued by a lion, which is promptly killed by Apelle and Oronte. Campaspe asks Apelle's pardon. She now realizes that he has loved her enough to give her up to Alessandro. She also realizes that Statira has not been her intentional rival. She orders Oronte, still disguised, to rush and save Statira from murder. Oronte leaves.

Sc. 5 (Nos. 80–86). Campaspe and Apelle profess their love for one another.

Sc. 6 (Nos. 87, 88). Perinto goes in search of Statira.

Sc. 7 (No. 89). Oronte informs Statira that she has been saved from death. Perinto enters saying that he has brought soldiers from Alessandro to guard Statira in her retreat.

Sc. 8 (Nos. 90–93). Oronte explains Campaspe's jealousy and the murder plot. Demetrio enters and confesses that it was he who tried to kill Statira, but that the heavens opened up when he was about to do it. Statira forgives both him and Campaspe.

Sc. 9 (Nos. 94–97). Apelle is delighted that all is well between him and Campaspe. Alessandro, as yet, is not certain of Statira's feelings toward him. He orders that the temple be made ready for nuptials, should Statira accept him.

Sc. 10 (Nos. 98, 99). Perinto rushes in to announce Statira's imminent arrival. Alessandro leaves to await her in the temple.

Sc. 11. (No. 100). Campaspe arrives and Perinto twits her about her aspirations to the throne. She answers that she loves nobody but Apelle. She also wishes to make amends to Statira.

Sc. 12 (Nos. 101, 102). Statira arrives and pardons Campaspe.

Sc. 13 (Nos. 103, 104). Demetrio, alone in the temple, swears that never again will he fall in love.

Sc. 14 (No. 105). Apelle, Perinto, and Alessandro are in the temple. Alessandro still is doubtful that Statira will accept him as a husband.

Sc. 15 (Nos. 106–110). Statira and Oronte enter. After much discussion, it is clear to all that they love each other. Alessandro blesses their marriage, sadly, and prepares to depart.

Sc. 16 (Nos. 111–117). Campaspe enters. Alessandro announces that not only is he giving Statira to Oronte, but also that he is abdicating his throne in favor of them. He is distraught. Oronte then breaks in saying that he cannot be responsible for such a noble sacrifice. Therefore, he will give up Statira to Alessandro in order that all may end well. Statira, after some hesitation, accepts this decision. Apelle and Campaspe will also be united. The goddess Diana appears and blesses both couples. The opera ends as Alessandro and Apelle sing the praises of their brides.

LA STATIRA

Interlocutori

Macedoni

Alessandro Magno, re de' Macedoni	[Soprano]
Campaspe, favorita di Alessandro	[Soprano]
Apelle, amante di Campaspe	[Tenore]
Demetrio, generale de' Macedoni, amante di Campaspe	[Basso]
Perinto, servo di corte	[Soprano]

Persiani

Statira, figlia di Dario, re de' Persiani, amante d'Oronte poi moglie d'Alessandro	[Alto]
Oronte, prencipe Persiano, amante di Statira sotto nome d'Elvio, mercante Armeno	[Tenore]

Balli

di Persiani
di Ninfe

La scena si finge in Damasco.

Mutazioni di Scene

Atto Primo

Campagna spaziosa in tempo di notte con luna
Padiglione di Dario
Sala regia con statue
Carcere ove dimorano gli avanzi dell'esercito Persiano con soldati prigionieri a sedere sovra li loro scudi, & armi rotte

Atto Secondo

Galleria di quadri
Sala regia con statue
Gruppo di monti con l'eremo di Statira e mausoleo di Dario

Atto Terzo

Caverna sotterranea
Bosco che discende all'eremo di Statira in una valle
Piazza della città con archi trionfali e palazzo regio
Tempio di Diana con vittime sopra gl'altari

1. Sinfonia
avanti l'alzar della tenda

35
40
soli
45
tutti
50
55
60

65
70
75
80
85
90

ATTO PRIMO

Scena i

Campagna con veduta in lontananza di collinette sotto le quali
sta nel sonno immerso l'esercito persiano;
cielo stellato con luna piena che fa distinguere la multitudine dei soldati
ed il real padiglione di Dario nel mezzo.

Oronte

2. *Recitativo accompagnato*

20
co-re a-man-te non co-no-sce ri-po-so, non co-no-sce ri-po-so un so-lo i-stan-te.
6 6 6 4 3

3. Aria

Grave con spirito
Oronte
cembalo
Continuo
Ho di
sel-ce la co-stan - - - za, son di mar - - mo, son di mar - - - - - - -
5
- - mo fra mar-ti - ri, fra mar-ti - - - - - - - - ri, fra mar - ti - - - - - - -
10
ri. Mi dà vi - ta la spe - ran-za, mi dà vi - ta la spe-ran-za e re - spi-ro con so-spi-ri, e re -
15
spi-ro con so-spi - - - - - - ri, e re - spi-ro con so-spi - - - - - - - ri.
Da capo
Segue il ritornello.

Ritornello
Violino I
Violino II
Viola
Continuo
Seconda stanza
Oronte
Continuo
Non ___ pro -
cu - ro di gio - i - - - - - re, ___ mi son dol - - - ci, mi son dol - - - - - - -
- - - ci le ca - te - ne, le ca - te - - - - - - - - ne, le ca - te - - - - - - -
ne. Non ri - cu - so di ___ sof - fri - re, non ri - cu - so di ___ sof - fri - re e son gra - te a me le pe - ne, e son

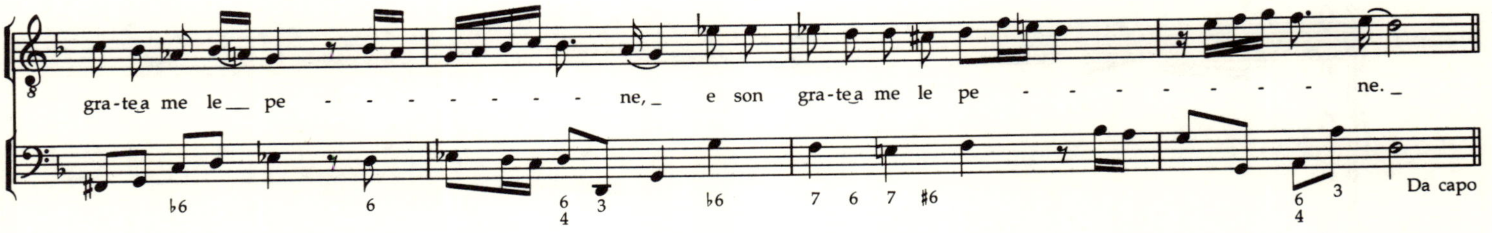

4. *Recitativo*

Suonano le trombe a guerra.

Scena ii

Si vedono tutte quelle collinette coperte dall'esercito dei
Macedoni che con lenta marcia sfilano alla volta dei
Persiani; Alessandro sopra il suo famoso Bucefalo alla testa dei suoi soldati,
ed Oronte che risveglia il campo di Dario.

Alessandro

5. *Aria*

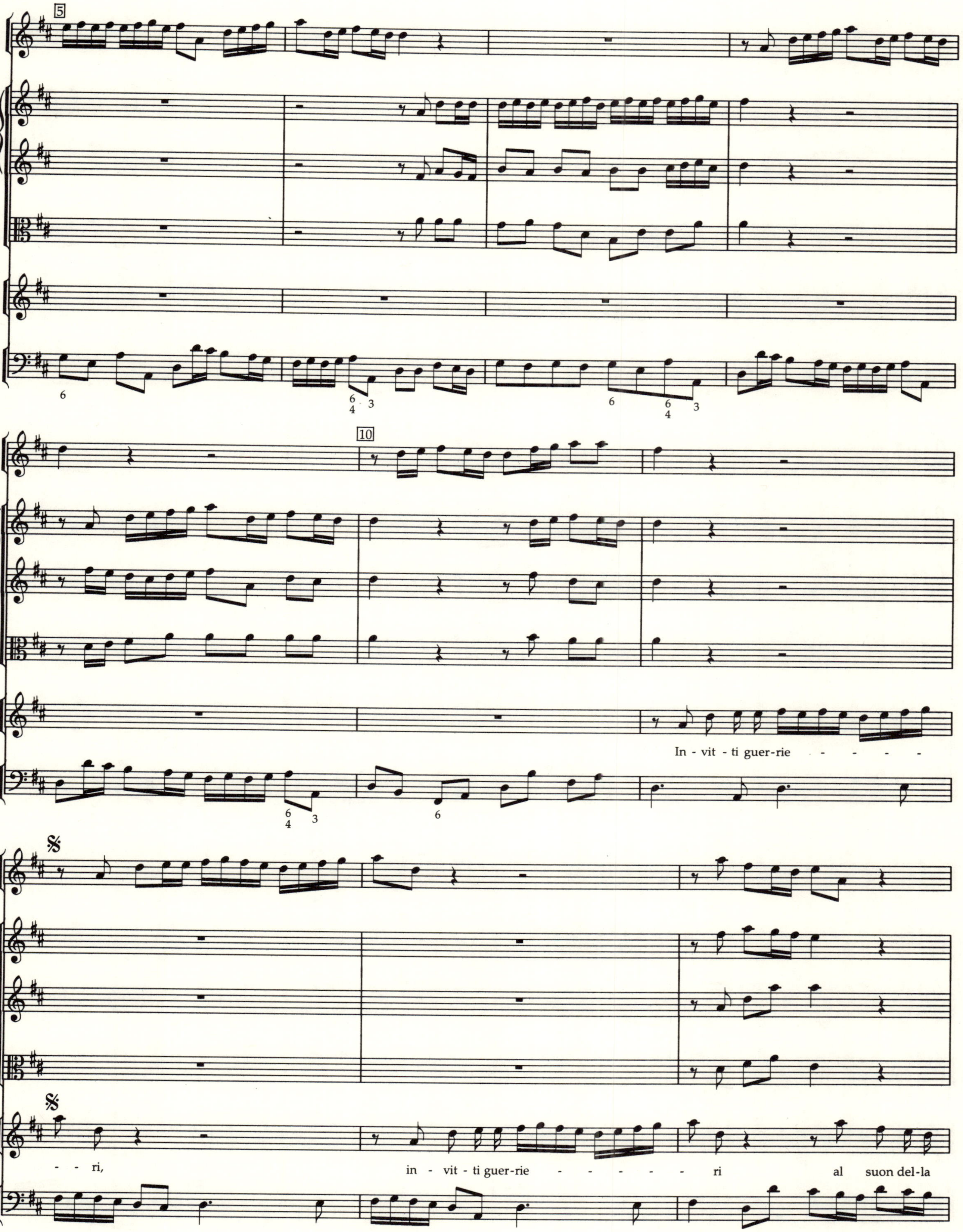
In - vit - ti guer-rie - - - - -
- - ri,
in - vit - ti guer-rie - - - - - - ri
al suon del-la

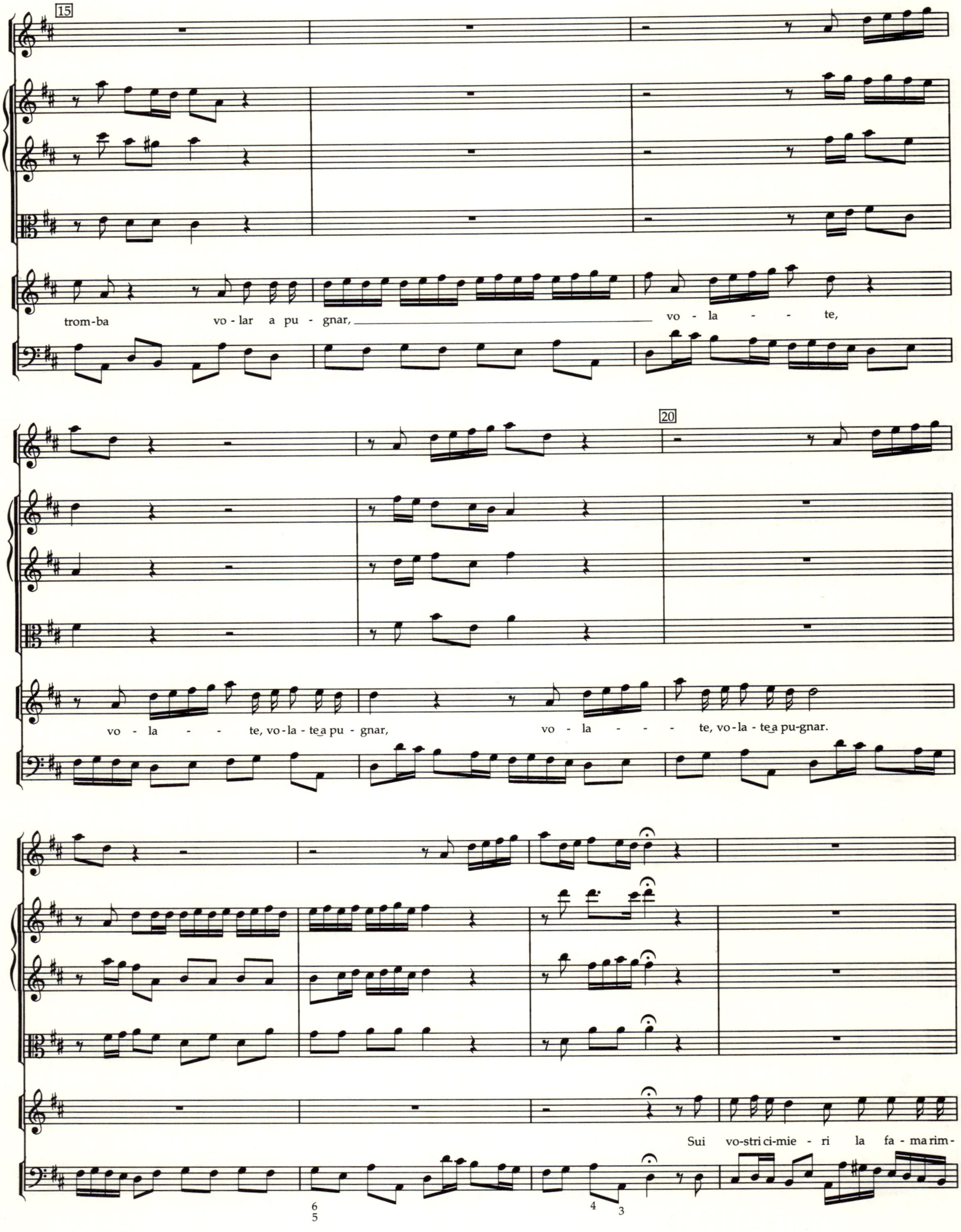
15
trom-ba vo-lar a pu-gnar, vo-la - - te,
20
vo-la - - te, vo-la-te͜ a pu-gnar, vo-la - - - te, vo-la-te͜ a pu-gnar.
Sui vo-stri ci-mie-ri la fa-ma rim-
6
5
4
3

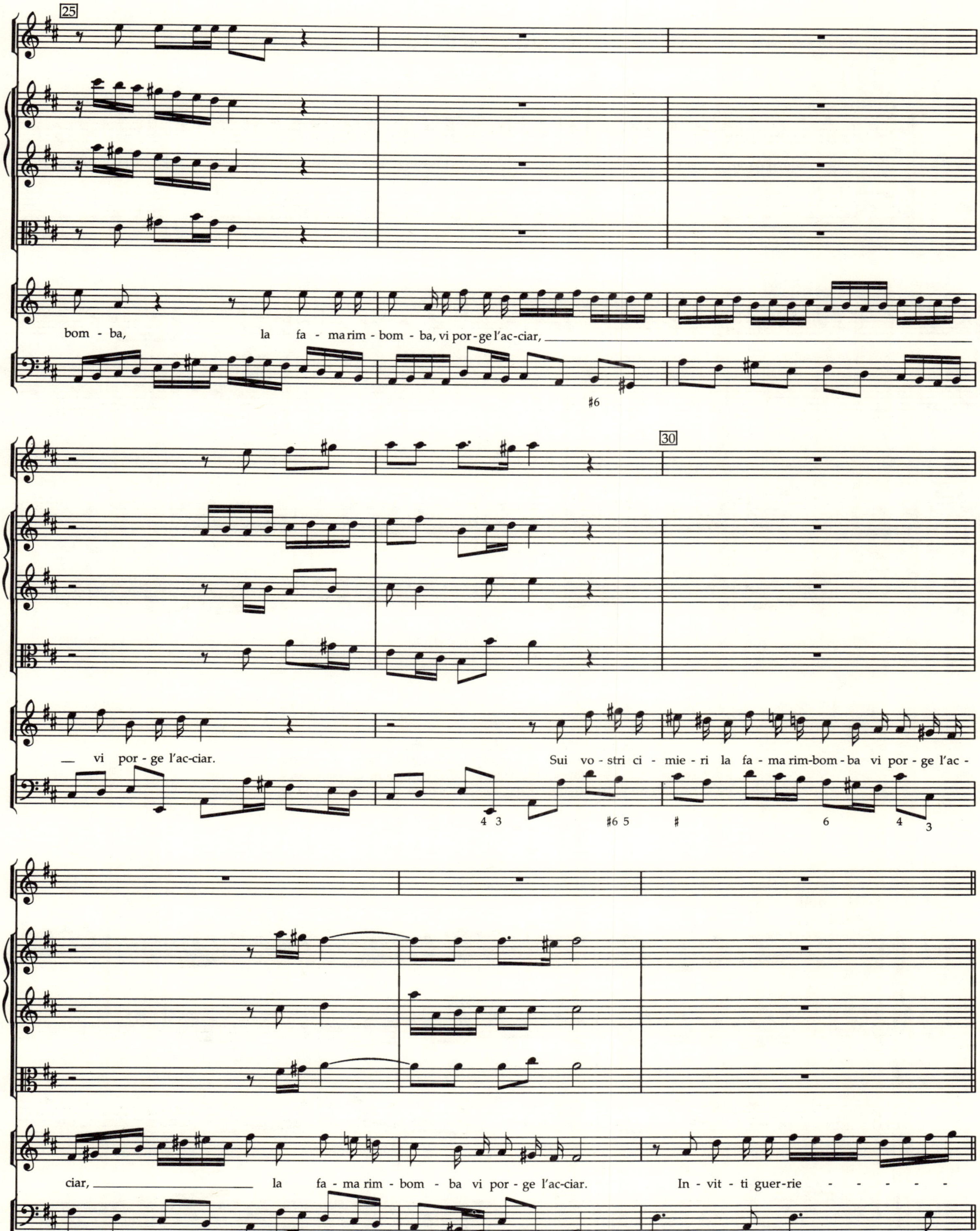
25
bom - ba, la fa - ma rim - bom - ba, vi por - ge l'ac - ciar,
♯6
30
— vi por - ge l'ac - ciar. Sui vo - stri ci - mie - ri la fa - ma rim - bom - ba vi por - ge l'ac -
4 3 ♯6 5 ♯ 6 4 3
ciar, la fa - ma rim - bom - ba vi por - ge l'ac - ciar. In - vit - ti guer - rie - - - - -
6
Dal segno
Segue Alessandro.

6. *Recitativo*

A suon di trombe si mette in battaglia l'esercito persiano.

Qui suonano le trombe a carica per la zuffa degli eserciti.
A suon di trombe e tamburi si getta Alessandro in mezzo ai nemici;
resta la vittoria ai Macedoni e vien preso il padiglione di Dario sul
quale vien posto Alessandro corteggiato dall'esercito vittorioso in trionfo con fanali accesi.

Qui suonano le trombe

7. *Aria*

5
10
Alessandro
Continuo
Poi - chè a - ve - te, _ va-ghe stel - le, _ va-ghe stel-le, poi - chè a - ve - te, _ va-ghe stel - le, _ va-ghe
15
stel - le, da - to _ lu - ce al mio va - lor, per _ far _ chia - re o - pre sì
tr
20
bel - le voi ce-de - te, voi ce - de - te al _ sol l'o-nor, voi ce -
25
de - te al _ sol l'o-nor, per _ far _ chia - re o - pre sì bel - le voi ce - de - te, voi ce-de - te al _ sol l'o-

Qui suonano le trombe ad aria.

Seconda ***stanza***

Segue la sinfonia di trombe.

8. Sinfonia di trombe nel trionfo d'Alessandro

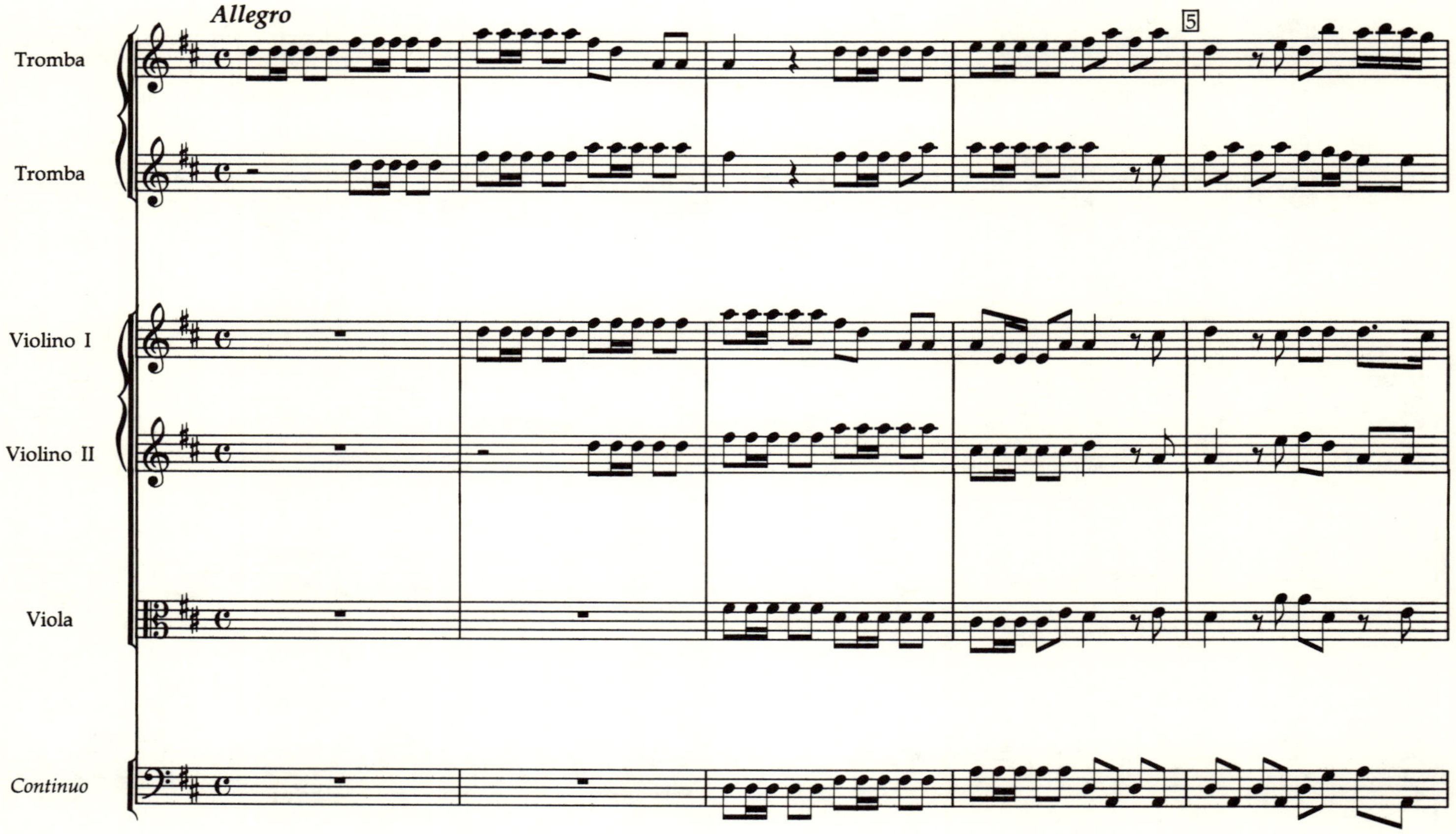

10
15
tr

Scena iii

Oronte solo

9. *Recitativo accompagnato*

10
fa - li al - lo - ri ro - tan - do ai dan - ni mie - i sem - pre, sem - pre ri - bel - le. Cru - do
15
cie - - lo, em - pio fa - to, i - ni - que stel - le
20

Re tra-fit - to, o - nor per -
du - to, o - nor per - du - to son le fu - rie, son le
fu - rie del cor mi - o, del cor mi - o, ma do - lor, ma do - lor più a-cer - bo e ri - o, più a-cer - bo e _
25
adagio
30
p
6
♯

Si replica il ritornello [measures 41-43] se bisogna.

Scena iv

Gran padiglione di Dario con letto e nel mezzo una lumiera;
Statira genuflessa in terra sopra il cadavere del padre che piange.

Statira

10. *Recitativo accompagnato*

11. *Recitativo*

pian - to? Di ca-te-ne ser - vi - li cin-ge-rò il piè. Sa - ran - no e - sca le mie bel - lez - ze di la-sci-vo ti -
ran - no. Ah fie-ra sor-te, per fi-ne a tan-to duol dam - mi la mor - - - - - - - - - - - - te.

Segue Statira l'aria con violini.

12. Aria

Largo assai
Violino I
Violino II
Viola
Statira
Continuo
solo
tutti
Sì, sì che la
mor-te in - vo - co, sì che la mor-te in - vo - co, mor-te deh vie-ni a me, vie - ni,

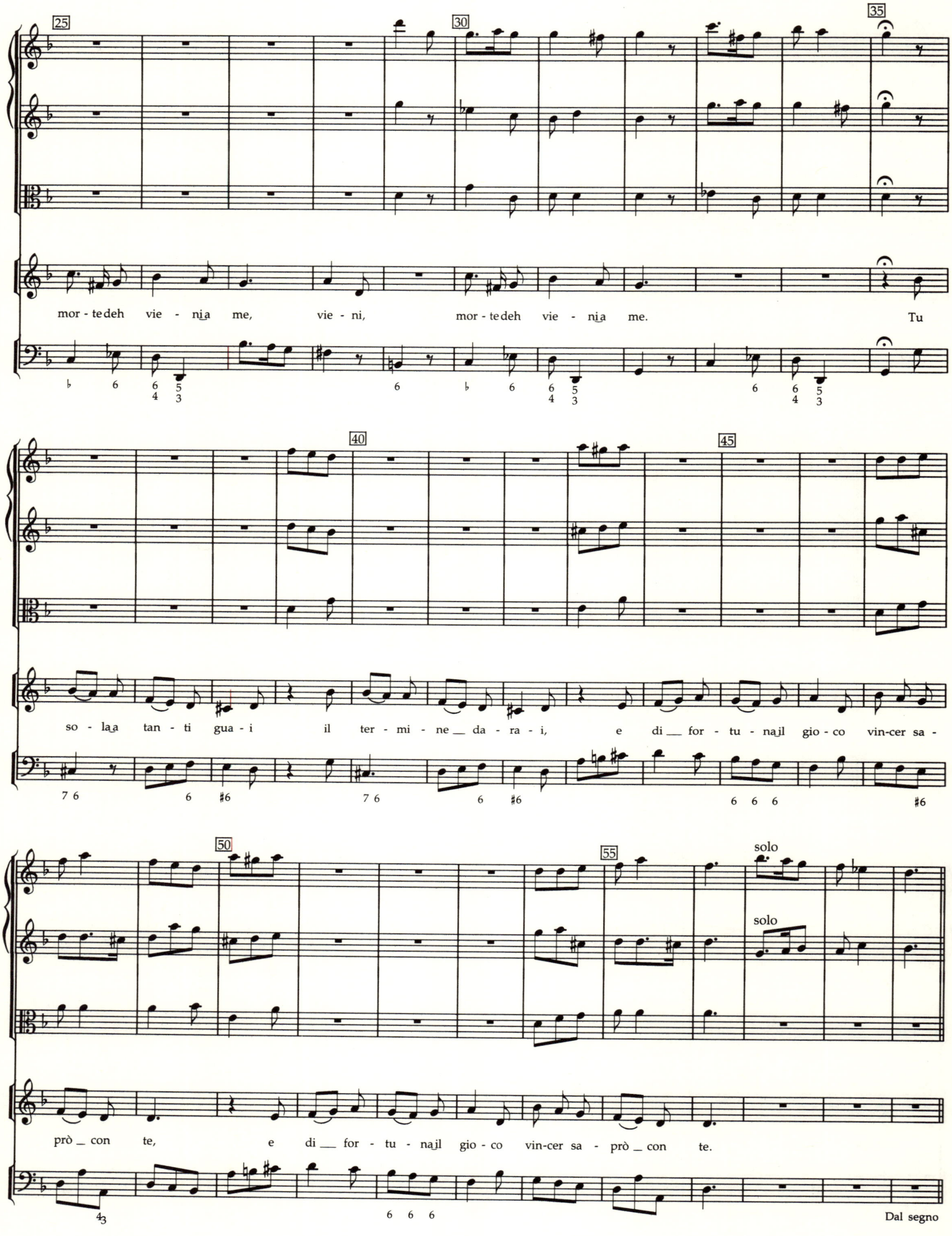
25
30
35
mor - te deh vie - ni a me, vie - ni, mor - te deh vie - ni a me. Tu
40
45
so - la a tan - ti gua - i il ter - mi - ne __ da - ra - i, e di __ for - tu - na il gio - co vin-cer sa -
50
55
solo
solo
prò __ con te, e di __ for - tu - na il gio - co vin-cer sa - prò __ con te.
Dal segno

Scena v

Demetrio e Perinto con soldati, e Statira sul letto in atto melanconico.

Demetrio, Perinto, Statira

13. Aria

14. *Recitativo*

15. Aria

Andante
Demetrio
Continuo
Con - so - la-ti non pian-ge-re, con -
so - la-ti non pian - ge-re, chè fran - ge-re po-trai l'a - spro de - stin, l'a - spro _ de - stin, l'a - spro _ de - stin, chè fran - ge-re po -
trai l'a - spro de-stin. Per vin - cer o-gni cor l'ar - co del dio d'a-mor, l'ar - co del dio d'a - mor si for -
- - - - - ma _ col suo crin, si for - - - - - - - - ma _ col suo crin.
Dal segno
Segue il ritornello.
Ritornello
Violino I
Violino II
Viola
Continuo

25
Seconda stanza
Statira
Al duol si è re-so im - mo - bi - le,
al duol si è re-so im - mo - bi - le il no - bi - le ben -
Continuo
30
chè tra - fit - to sen, tra - fit - to sen, tra - fit - to sen, il no - bi - le ben - chè tra - fit - to
sen. Con per - fi-de ri - tor - te non sa per - ver - sa sor - te far l'al - ma ve - nir men,
35
far l'al - ma ve - nir men, con per - fi-de ri - tor - te non sa per - ver - sa sor - te far l'al - ma ve - nir
40
men, l'al - - - - - - ma ve - nir men.
Al duol si è re - so im -
Dal segno

16. *Recitativo*

17. Aria

20
nè fo tor - to___ a___ gio - ven - tù, a___ gio - ven - tù. Se - guo il dol - ce,
25
30
se - guo il dol - ce e non l'a - ma - ro, cer - co quel che al - et - ta più,
35 solo
40
tutti
se - guo il dol - ce non l'a - ma - ro, cer - co quel___ che al - let - ta più.
Da capo

Scena vi

Giardinetto che viene bagnato da una picciola lingua di mare.

Campaspe sola

18. *Recitativo*

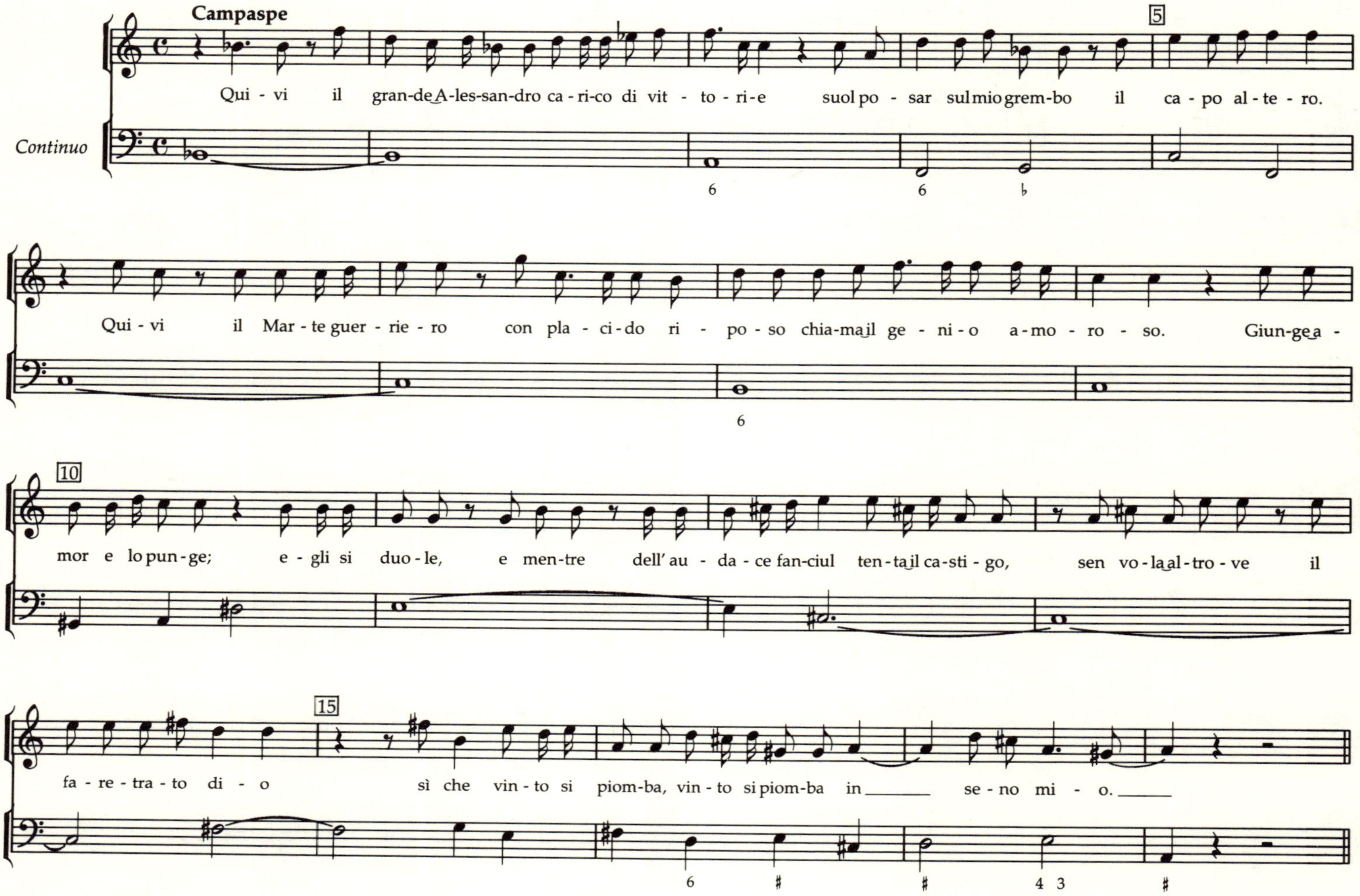
Campaspe
Continuo
Qui - vi il gran-de A-les-san-dro ca-ri-co di vit - to - ri-e suol po - sar sul mio grem-bo il ca - po al - te - ro.
Qui - vi il Mar - te guer - rie - ro con pla - ci-do ri - po - so chia-ma il ge - ni - o a - mo - ro - so. Giun-ge a -
mor e lo pun - ge; e - gli si duo - le, e men - tre dell' au - da - ce fan-ciul ten - ta il ca-sti - go, sen vo - la al - tro - ve il
fa - re - tra - to di - o sì che vin - to si piom-ba, vin - to si piom-ba in se - no mi - o.

19. Aria

Allegro
Campaspe
Continuo
Bel-tà che pia - ce,
bel - tà che pia - ce al cor di ge - lo com-par-te ar - dor, com-par

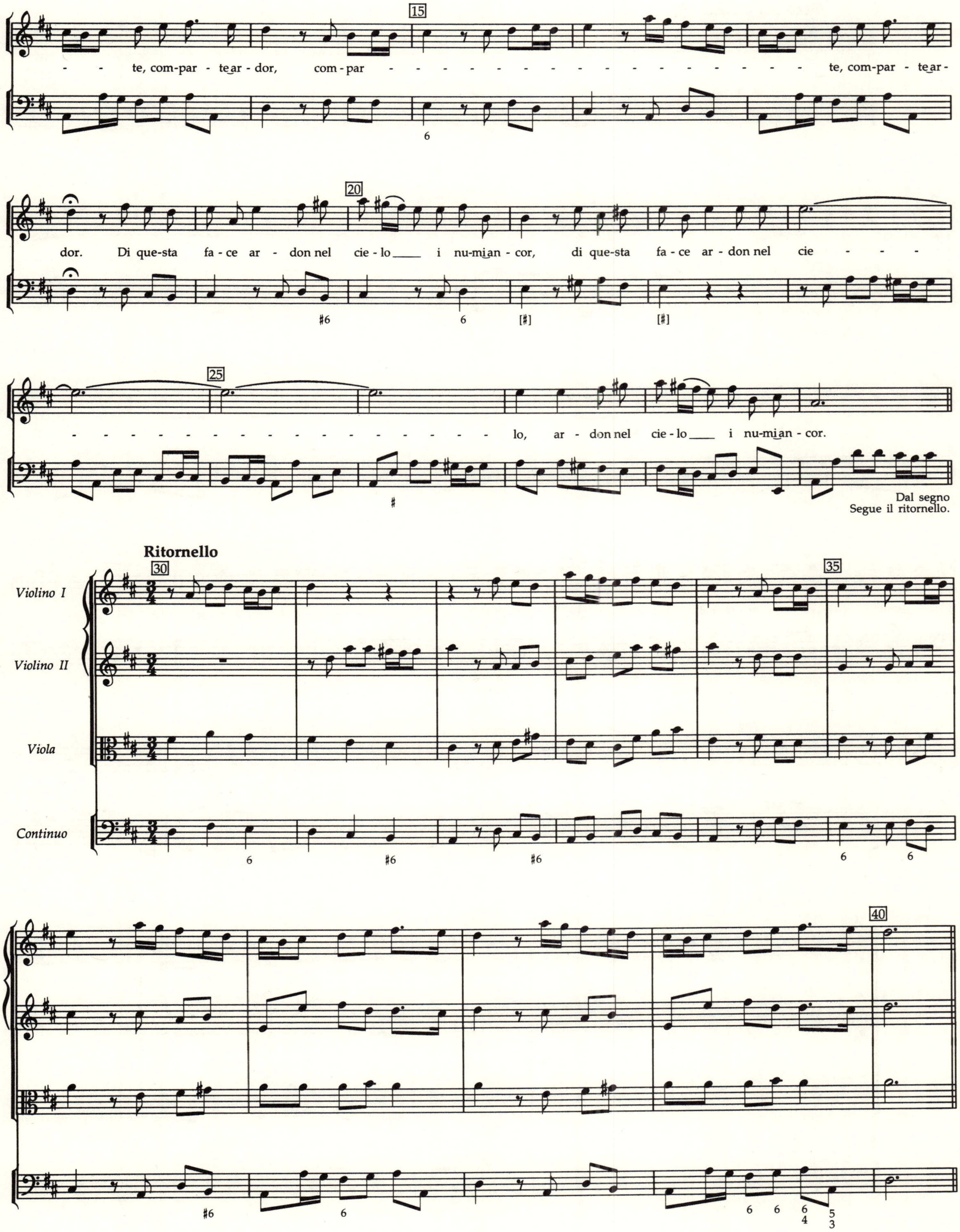
15
- - te, com-par - te ar - dor, com - par - - - - - - - - - - - - - - - - - te, com-par - te ar -
6
20
dor. Di que-sta fa - ce ar - don nel cie - lo i nu-mi an - cor, di que-sta fa - ce ar - don nel cie - - - -
#6 6 [#] [#]
25
- - - - - - - - - - - - - - - - - - - lo, ar - don nel cie - lo i nu-mi an - cor.
#
Dal segno
Segue il ritornello.
Ritornello
30
35
Violino I
Violino II
Viola
Continuo
6 #6 #6 6 6
40
#6 6 6 6 6 4 5 3

Seconda stanza
Campaspe
Continuo
45
Vol-to che al-let - ta,
vol-to che al-let - ta dal ciglio ar-cie-ro vi-bra lo stral, lo stral,
50
vi-bra lo stral, lo stral, vi-bra lo
55
stral. Dol-ce sa - et-ta, col - po se - ve-ro, pia-ga mor - tal, dol-ce sa - et-ta, col-po se - ve - - - -
60
ro, pia - ga mor - tal, pia-ga mor - tal.
65
Dal segno
Segue il ritornello.
Ritornello
70
75
Violino I
Violino II
Viola
Continuo

Scena vii

Campaspe assisa in una massa di rose; Apelle, e Oronte travestito d'Armeno.

20. *Recitativo*

Apelle
Oronte
Com-pa-ti-sco il tuo ca-so, El-vio in-no-cen-te, ma non te-mo. La sor-te mi spin-se ver Da - ma-sco, men-tre Al-les-san-dro, il vin-ci-
Continuo
tor del mon-do, Da-rio scon-fis - se e ap-pe - na sal-vai la vi - ta.
Apelle
Mia sa-rà la cu - ra di tua sa - lu - te.
Oronte
An - co - ra.
Apelle
Che?
Oronte
So - spi - ro.
Apelle
La li - ber - tà?
Oronte
Non que-sto.
Apelle
Le per-du - te ric - chez-ze?
Oronte
Es - se-re am-mes-so ad in - chi-nar Sta - ti - ra, per - ciò quest' al-ma mi - a so-lo so-spi-ra.
Apelle
Dif - fi - ci - le è l'im-pre-sa.
Oronte
E chi tel vie - ta?
Apelle
d'A-les-san-dro la cu - ra, men-tre già fat-to di Sta - ti - ra a-man-te, sua spo-sa e sua re - i - na og - gi far la de-sti-na.
Campaspe
Che re - i - na, che spo-sa?
Apelle
Scu-sa, bel-la Cam - pa - spe l'er-ror del

25
Campaspe
guar-do. O-mai sve-la-mi qual re-i-na, qual spo-sa si de-sti-na al se-no d'A-les-san-dro.
Apelle
O-pra fu que-sta del sa-ga-ce pen-
30
sier che te de-si-a. In-nal-zai le bel-lez-ze del-la va-ga stra-nie-ra, e con fe-li-ce e-ven-to al nuo-vo fuo-co, in-ten-to
35
Sta-ti-ra a lui, Cam-pa-spe a me.
Campaspe
Che a-scol-to? Em-pio, son que-sti i se-gni dell' a-mor, del-la fè che mi giu-ra-sti?
Oronte
Dis-
40
cor-die for-tu-na-te.
Apelle
An-zi, per-chè t'a-do-ro o-pro in tal gui-sa.
Campaspe
A-scol-ta, da me, da que-sto co-re ven-det-ta a-
45
spet-ta e non spe-rar a-mo-re.
Apelle
Per-chè?
Campaspe
Già son di sco-glio a chi mi to-glie e la co-ro-na e il so-glio.
Apelle
D'A-les-san-dro al-le
50
pian-te tor-ne-rò sup-pli-can-te, par-le-rò di Cam-pa-spe, ri-get-te-rò Sta-ti-ra.
Oronte
In-na-mo-ra-to cor, o-mai re-spi-ra.
55
Campaspe
Van-ne, che que-sto so-lo può fre-nar il mio sde-gno, ne vin-cer il ri-gor che in me s'a-du-na spe-ra, che con Vir-tù, Tem-po e For-tu-na.
60
Segue con violini.

21. *Aria*

Moderato
Violino I
Violino II
Viola
Campaspe
Continuo
Spez - za l'ar - co, spez - - - - - - - - za l'ar - co cie - co Di - o se non
hai d'o - ro lo stral,
se non ha - i d'o - ro lo stral, se non ha - i d'o - ro lo stral.
5

10
solo
Nel_ mio_ pet-to vi-le af-fet-to non può far col-po fa-tal,
tutti
tutti
tutti
15
non può far col-po fa-tal. Nel_ mio_ pet-to vi-le af-fet-to non può far col-po fa-
tal,
non può far col-po fa-tal.
Da capo

Scena viii

Oronte, Apelle

22. *Recitativo*

23. Aria

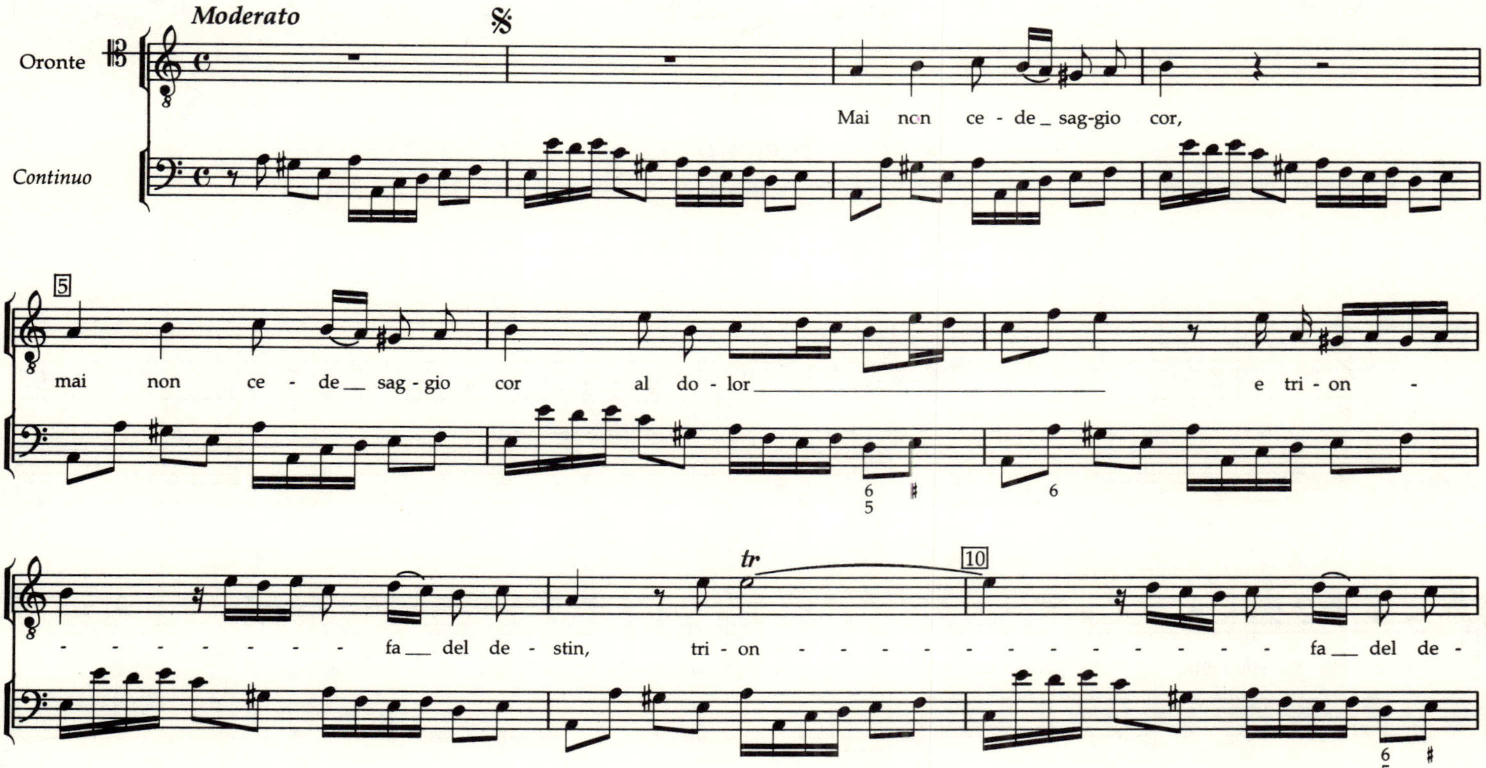

Scena ix

Apelle solo

24. *Recitativo*

25. Aria

Andante
Violino I
Violino II
Apelle
Continuo
Mi con - si - glio col mio co - re ed _ il cor, ed _ il cor dub - bio - so sta, dub - bio - so sta, dub - bio - so sta, dub - bio - so sta.
Non _ ho cer - to che il _ do - lo - re del - la

per - sa li - ber - tà. Non ho cer - to che il do - lo - re
del - la per - sa li - ber - tà. Mi con -
Dal segno
Seconda stanza
Violino I
Violino II
Apelle
Continuo
Cer - co in - va - no dal pen - sie - re il ri - pie - go, il ri - pie - go per

80
85
— gio - ir, il ri - pie - go___ per__ gio - ir, per_____ gio - ir, il ri - pie - go___ per__ gio - ir,
90
95
s'il _ pa - la - re___ ed il __ ta - ce - re___ mi con - dan - na -
100
105
- no a sof - frir, s'il par - la - re___ ed il ta - ce - re___
110
115
mi con - dan - na - - no a sof - frir. Cer - co in -
Dal segno

Scena x

Carcere nel mezzo del quale si vede in alto catafalco il cadavere di Dario con al piede una catena, numero grande di soldati persiani fra ceppi; Statira con abito nero in atto lagrimosa.

26. *Recitativo*

27. Aria

I violini suonino staccato e grave

po di tua ma-e-stà,
un lam - - - - - - po di tua ma-e-stà,
Quel af - fron - to che Da - rio ri - ce - ve dal tuo brac - cio pu -
ni - re si de - ve, e fia giu - sto de - sta - re il ri - go - re con chi
te - co ri - bel - le si fa, con chi te - co ri - bel - le si fa.
Da capo

Scena xi

Alessandro, Demetrio, Perinto, Statira vicino al catafalco.

28. *Recitativo*

Perinto
Continuo
Si-gnor, quan-to m'im - po-se De-me-tri-o il tuo gran du-ce pron-ta-men-te e-se - gui - i. Le fred-de mem-bra ec-co di Da-ri-o
ed i - vi mi-ra la fi-glia, e le re-li-quie vi - li dei Per-sia-ni guer-rie-ri ve-di qui in-tor-no lan-guir in ser-vi - tù.
Alessandro
Trop-po, trop-po ri-go-re.
Demetrio
A tan-to or-go-glio, a tan - to fa - sto e - gua - le par - mi, gran Re, la pe - na.
Alessandro
In me pre - va - le la cle-men-za e non l'i - ra,
chè il più va - go dia-de - ma di cui va un crin tri-on - fa - to - re ac - cin - to è la pie - tà del vin - ci - to - re al vin - to.

Segue l'aria d'Alessandro con violini.

29. Aria

Largo
Violino I
Violino II
Alessandro
Continuo
La cle - men - za nel cord'un re - gnan - te,
la cle - men - za nel cor d'un re -

gnan - te è di Fe - bo l'i - ma - - - - - go ve - ra - ce,
10
è di Fe - bo l'i - ma - - - go ve - ra - - ce. Che non bruc - cia nè fio - ri nè pian - te, ma le
15
scal - - - - - da con pla - ci - da fa -
20
- - - ce, con pla - ci - da fa - - - - - - - - - - - - - ce. La cle - men - za nel cord' un re -
Dal segno

30. *Recitativo*

que-sta A-les-san-dro a me gra-zia non ne-ga. In re-mo-ta fo-re-sta o-ve rag-gio di Fe-bo mai giun-se a fu-gar
35
l'om-bre, u-ni-ta al ge-ni-to-re bra-mo pas-sar pian-gen-do i gior-ni e l'o-re.
Alessandro
Trop-po al duol t'ab-ban-do-ni.
Statira
È que-sto il mio de-si-re.
40
Alessandro
Ta-lor vin-cer se stes-sa è vir-tù.
Statira
Non e-spres-sa dai la-men-ti, la pe-na ve-ra pe-na non è. Chè se el-la pre-me un cor che ha sen-so,
45
ei ne so-spi-ra e ge-me.
Alessandro
Com-pia-cer-ti ri-sol-vo e ti da-rà con-si-glio tua Vir-tù nel scher-nir Tem-po e For-tu-na.
50
Statira
Co-sì mo-stri A-les-san-dro quan-to giu-sti al tuo crin sia-no gli al-lo-ri, se ac-qui-sti al tuo gran so-glio col bran-do i re-gni
55
e con le gra-zie i co-ri.

31. Aria

Largo
Statira
Continuo
Pre-pa-ta-te-vi miei lu-mi,
pre-pa-ra-te-vi miei lu-mi tut-ti lie-ti, tut-ti lie-ti a la-gri-mar, a la-gri-
mar, tut-ti lie-ti a la-gri-mar, a la-gri-mar. So-la, so-la
pian-ge-rò, so-la, so-la pian-ge-rò, nè sa-prò che nel duo-lo, che nel duo-lo re-spi-
rar, nè sa-prò che nel duol-lo, che nel duo-lo re-spi-rar.
Da capo
Segue il ritornello.
Ritornello
Violino I
Violino II
Viola
Continuo

Scena xii

Alessandro, Demetrio, Perinto

32. *Recitativo*

33. Aria

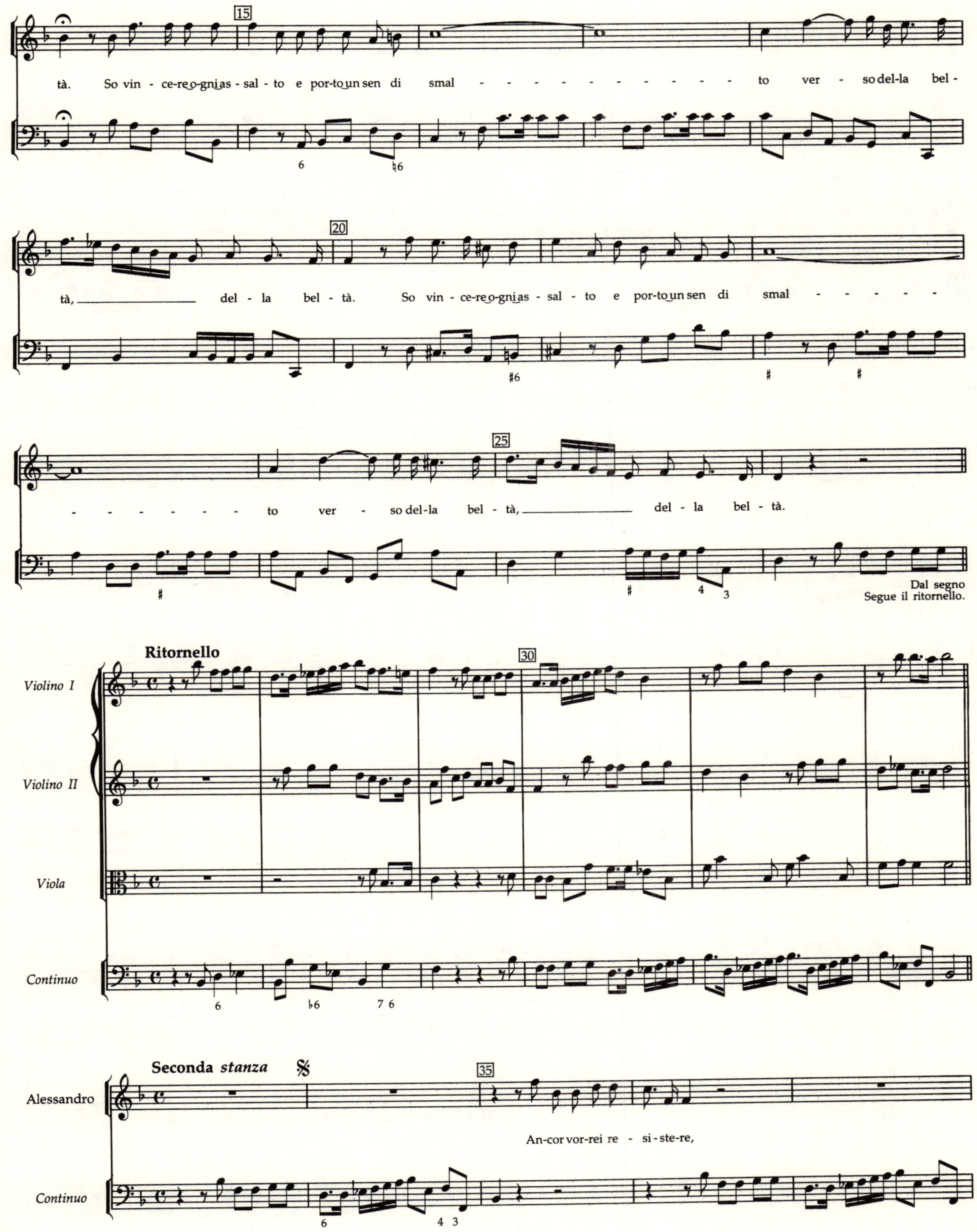

15
tà. So vin - ce-re o-gni as - sal - to e por-to un sen di smal - - - - - - - - - - - - - to ver - so del-la bel -
20
tà, del - la bel - tà. So vin - ce-re o-gni as - sal - to e por-to un sen di smal - - - - -
25
- - - - - - - to ver - so del-la bel - tà, del - la bel - tà.
Dal segno
Segue il ritornello.
Ritornello
30
Violino I
Violino II
Viola
Continuo
Seconda stanza
35
Alessandro
An-cor vor-rei re - si-ste-re,
Continuo

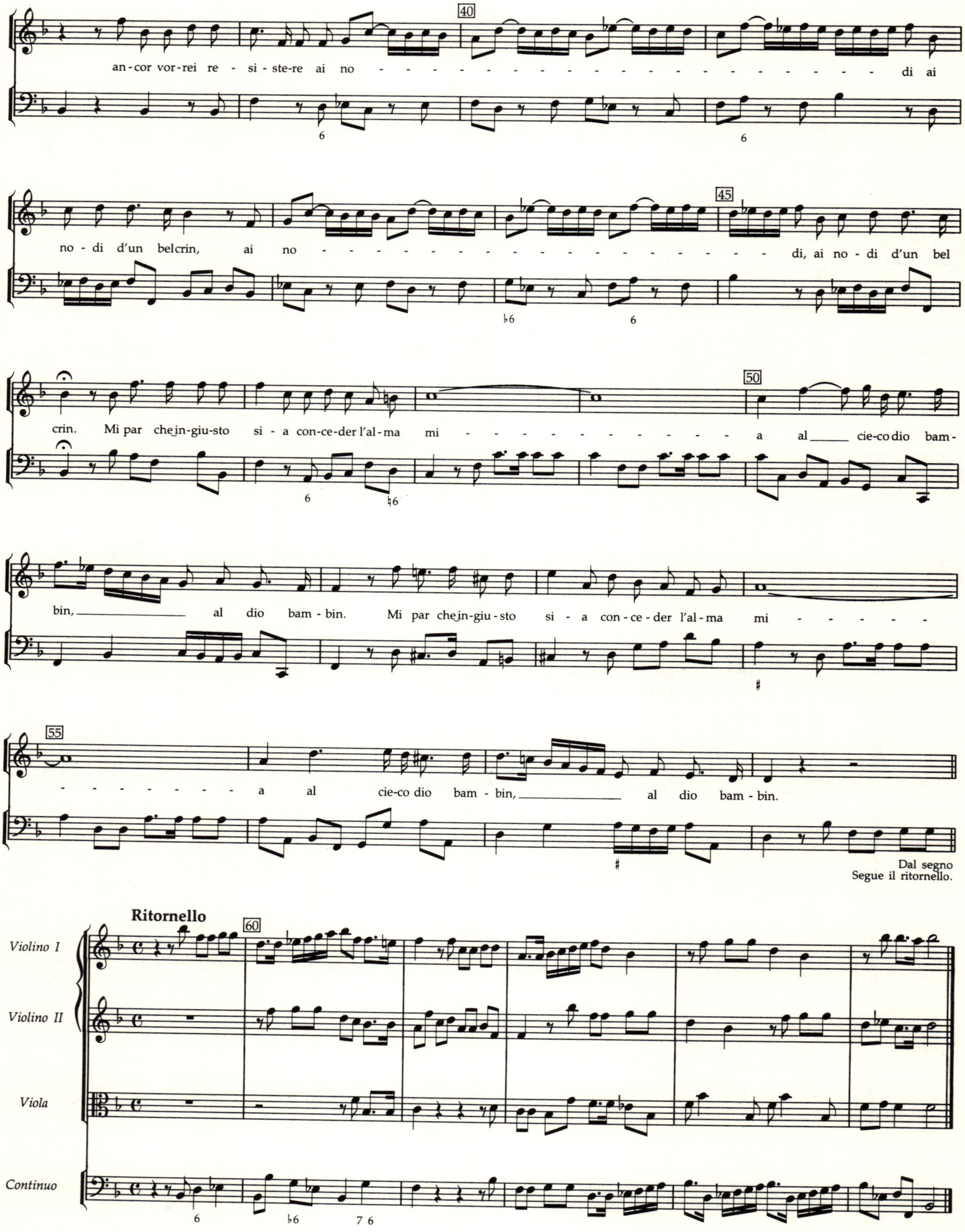
40
an-cor vor-rei re - si-ste-re ai no - - - - - - - - - - - - - - - - - - - di ai
no - di d'un belcrin, ai no - - - - - - - - - - - - - - - - - - di, ai no - di d'un bel
45
crin. Mi par che in-giu-sto si - a con-ce-der l'al-ma mi - - - - - - - - - - - - - a al cie-co dio bam-
50
bin, al dio bam - bin. Mi par che in-giu-sto si - a con - ce - der l'al - ma mi - - - - - -
55
- - - - - - - - a al cie-co dio bam - bin, al dio bam - bin.
Dal segno
Segue il ritornello.
Ritornello
60
Violino I
Violino II
Viola
Continuo

Scena xiii

Demetrio, Perinto

34. *Recitativo*

Demetrio
Continuo
In-dar-no m'af-fa - ti - co d'in-vo-gliar per Sta - ti - ra il re-gio co - re. E la va-na spe - ran - za d'ot-te-ner in tal
gui - sa l'a-do-ra - ta Cam - pa - spe par che al-tro - ve sen vo - li.
Perinto
An - cor non de - vi di-spe-rar - ne l'e-ven - to.
Ve-sti-re-mo l'Ar-me - no da sil-ve-stre pa-sto - re, e la stra-nie-ra prin-ci - pes-sa Sta-ti - ra nel so-li-ta-rio spe-co, e-sor-te-rà bra-
ma-re il re-gio no-da sì che rie-da al-la cor - te e A - les-san-dro col suo vol-to al-let - ti.
Demetrio
Che te ne par? Non sprez-zo
il pru-den-te con-si - glio. In te, in te con - fi-do, Pe-rin - to, di pro - var dol - ce Cu - pi - do.

Segue l'aria Demetrio con violini.

35. *Aria*

Moderato
Violino I
Violino II
Viola
Demetrio
Continuo
Vo-glio, vo-glio spe - ra-re dal dio d'a - mo-re qual - che mer - cè. Vo-glio, vo - glio spe -

ra - re___ dal_ dio_ d'a - mo - re___ qual-che mer - cè.
solo
tutti
Chè la - gri - ma - re fi-do‿a-ma - to - re sem - - - - - - - pre, sem - pre non dè.
Chè la - gri - ma - re___ fi-do‿a-ma - to - re___ sem - - - - - - - pre, sem - pre non dè.
Da capo

Scena xiv

Perinto

36. *Recitativo*

Perinto
Per-si-a-ni, an-cor tar-da-te a pro-var vo-stra sor-te. Sù gio-i-te, go-de-te, la-scia-te le ri-tor-te.
Continuo

37. Aria

Allegro assai
Perinto
Continuo
Bi-so-gna pian-ge-re men_ che_ si_ può, men che si può, men che si può, bi-so-gna pian-ge-re men_ che_ si_ può, chè trop-po la-bi-le sen_ fug-ge il_ dì. E quan-do il giu-bi-lo da noi spa-rì, che sia re-tro-gra-do nol_ cre-de-rò, chè trop-po la-bi-le sen_ fug-ge il_ dì. E quan-do il giu-bi-lo da_ noi_ spa-rì, che sia re-tro-gra-do nol_ cre-de-rò, nol_ cre-de-rò.

Da capo
Segue il ritornello.

Ritornello quale servirà ancora per il ballo

ATTO SECONDO

Scena i

Stanza di pittura con i ritratti di Statira e Campaspe.

Alessandro, Apelle

38. *Recitativo*

39. *Duetto*

Largo
Violino I
Violino II
Viola
Alessandro
Se t'of-fen-do mi per - do - na ca-ra gio-ia del_mio cor.
Apelle
Se t'of-fen-do mi per - do - na ca-ra gio-ia del_mio
Continuo
5
p
Se t'of - fen - do mi per don - a ca - ra gio - ia__ del_ mio
cor. Mi per - do - na ca - ra gio - ia__ del_ mio cor, ca - ra

10
p
p
p
cor, ca - ra, ca - ra, ca - ra gio - ia del mio cor, ca - ra gio - ia del mio cor. In -
gio - ia, ca - ra, ca - ra, ca - ra gio - ia del mio cor, ca - ra gio - ia del mio cor.
col - pa quel cru - do, quel cru - do fan - ciul - lo d'a - mor che ar - ma - to ed i - gnu - do
In - col - pa quel cru - do, quel cru - do fan - ciul - lo d'a - mor che ar - ma - to ed i -

15
mi por - ge, mi por - - ge do - lor. In - col - pa quel cru - do, quel
gnu - do mi por - ge do - lor, mi por - ge do - lor. In - col - pa quel cru - do, quel
20
cru - do fan - ciul - lo d'a - mor che ar - ma - to ed i - gnu - do mi por - ge do - lor. Se t'of - fen - do mi per -
cru - do fan - ciul - lo d'a - mor che ar - ma - to ed i - gnu - do mi por - ge do - lor.
Dal segno

Scena ii

Campaspe, Alessandro, Apelle

40. *Recitativo*

Campaspe
Continuo
Da che car-co d'al - lo - ri con per-sia-ne ca - te-ne u - ni - sti al-tre re - a - mi al tuo gran so-glio, Si-gnor, fuor dell' u -
sa-to tar-do a me rie - di? For-se il tuo gran co-re im-mer-so è co-sì nei tri - on - fi che di - sprez-za que-sta un dì so-spi - ra-ta mia bel-lez-za.

41. Aria

Moderato
Campaspe
Continuo
Do-vrò per mia ri - va-le, do-vrò per mia re -
va - le o - diar, o - diar la tua vir - tù, o - diar, o - diar la tua vir -
tù. Se fa che il cor re - a - le, se fa che il cor re - a - le a me, a me non tor - ni più, non tor - ni
più, non tor - ni più, se fa che il cor re - a - le a me non tor - ni più, non tor - ni più.
Dal segno
Segue il ritornello.

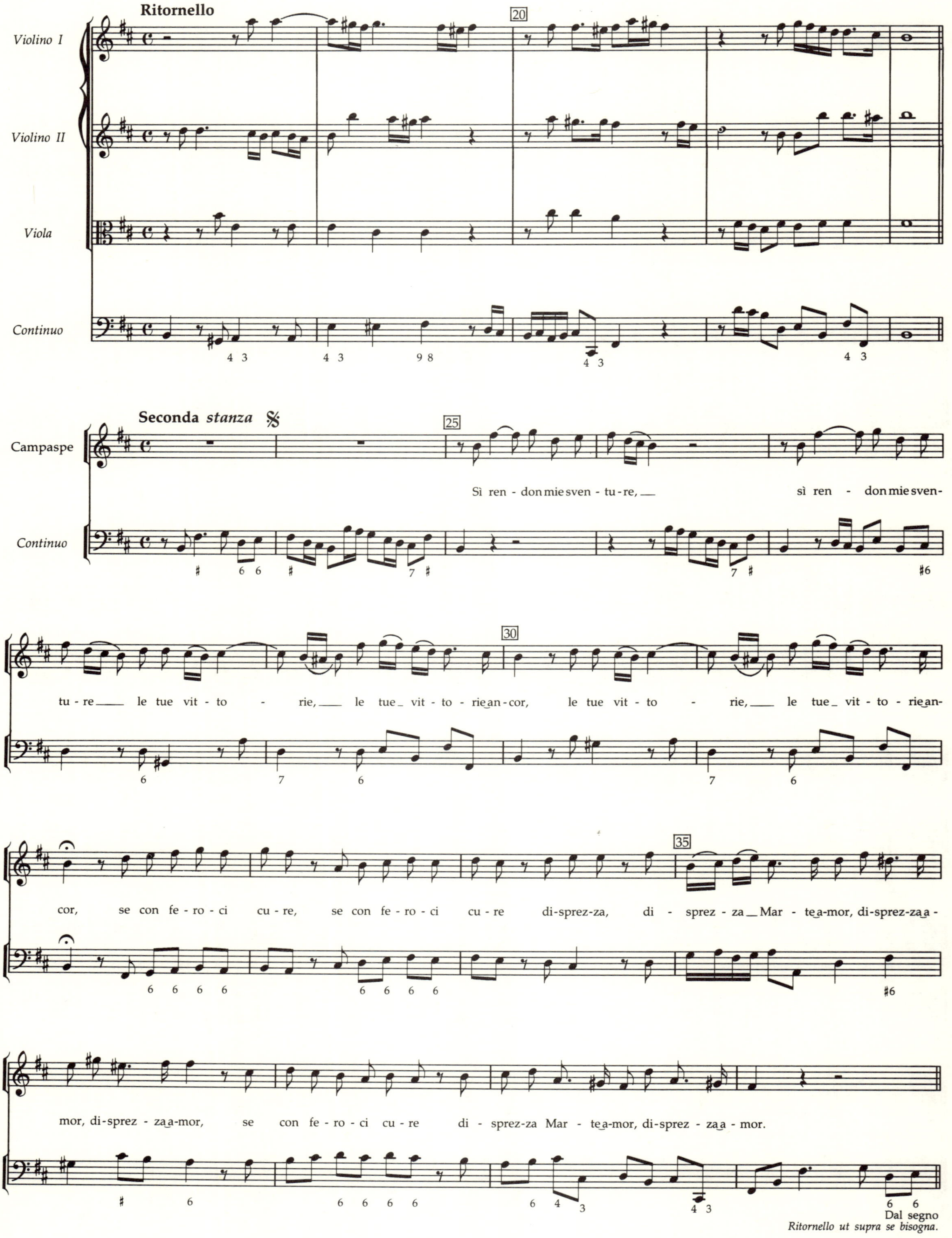

Ritornello
Violino I
Violino II
Viola
Continuo
20
4 3
4 3
9 8
4 3
4 3
Seconda stanza
Campaspe
Continuo
25
Sì ren - don mie sven - tu - re, __ sì ren - don mie sven-
tu - re __ le tue vit - to - rie, __ le tue _ vit - to - rie an - cor, le tue vit - to - rie, __ le tue _ vit - to - rie an-
30
cor, se con fe - ro - ci cu - re, se con fe - ro - ci cu - re di - sprez - za, di - sprez - za __ Mar - te a - mor, di - sprez - za a -
35
mor, di - sprez - za a - mor, se con fe - ro - ci cu - re di - sprez - za Mar - te a - mor, di - sprez - za a - mor.
Dal segno
Ritornello ut supra se bisogna.

42. *Recitativo*

43. Aria

Moderato
Apelle
Continuo
Es - ser po - trai cru - de - le, cru -
de - le, cru - de - le con chi lan - gue per - te, lan - - - - - - - - - - - gue per te? Che
gio - va es - ser fe - de - le, che gio - va es - ser fe - de - le sen - za spe - rar mer - cè, sen - za spe - rar mer - cè,
sen - za spe - rar mer - cè?
Andante
La cru - del - tà, la cru - del - tà, a chi ti do - na il cor, a chi ti do - na il cor vir - tù non è.
Moderato
Es - ser po - trai cru - de - le,
cru - de - le, cru - de - le con chi lan - gue per - te, lan - - - - - - - - - gue per te, con
chi lan - - - - - - gue, lan - gue per te, con chi lan - - - - - - - gue, lan - gue per te?
Segue il ritornello.

Ritornello
35
Violino I
Violino II
Viola
Continuo
40
p

Scena iii

Statira, Alessandro, Campaspe

44. *Recitativo*

Statira
Continuo
L'a-ver sciol-ti dai cep-pi i miei guer-rie-ri, O Si-re, del ge-ni-tor e-stin-to la-sciár-mi il ca-ro
5
pe-gno, con-ser-var-mi la vi-ta e del mio pian-to sen-tir pie-tà, fur o-pre de-gne di te; ma que-sta di per-met-ter ch'io
10
pos-sa en-tro ro-mi-ta stan-za go-der i gior-ni quie-ti o-gni al-tra a-van-za. Tu ri-man-ti al-le pal-me, e se lin-gua se-

15
pol - ta en-tro all' o-bli - o non da fia-to al-la fa-ma, fa - rò che nel-le sel - ve sen-tan le glo-rie tu - e pa -
Alessandro
20
Campaspe
sto-ri e bel-ve. Prin-ci-pes-sa, sol te-mo nel se-gui-re tua vo-glia e-ser-ci-tar at-to ti - ran-no. È dol-ce quel do-lor che si
Statira
25
Campaspe
bra-ma, e se chie-sto s'ot-tien, gra-zia si chia-ma. Bel - la, del gra-to uf-fi-ci-o mol-to ti de-vo. An-co-ra il pen-sier non ri-sol-ve
Alessandro
30
Campaspe
Alessandro
Statira
e s'ab-ban-do-na? Sta-ti-ra a te si de-ve o-gni fa-vor, ma... Co-me, vuoi man-car-le di fè? Pria mo-rir vo-glio. Par-to.
Alessandro
Statira
Alessandro
Allegro
35
No, an-cor. Per-chè? Mi dai cor-do-glio ma re-si - sta que - sto co - - - - -
40
Statira
Alessandro
Largo
re nè si do - ni a vi - le a - mor. Par-to a-dun-que. Nè an - cor, chè puoi far me - no per que-sto se - no di non par -
Campaspe
45
Statira
Alessandro
tir. Ti-ran-no ge-lo - si - a, mi fai mo - rir. Sper-giu-ro tu di - mo-stri se più re - si - sti. Hai vin-to.
Aria con violini.

45. *Aria*

Allegro
Violino I
Violino II
Viola
Alessandro
Continuo
Sof - fri - rò, sof - fri - rò tan - to do - lo - re, tan - to do - lo -
re per di - fen - de - re, per di - fen -
- - de - re l'o - nor. Sof - fri - rò

tan - to do - lo - re per di - fen - - - - - - de - re l'o - nor.
15
20
Ma re - si - sta que - sto co - - - - re, re - si - sta que - sto co - - - - re nè si do -
25
ni a vi - le a - mor, nè si do - ni a vi - le a - mor.

Scena iv

Statira, Campaspe

46. *Recitativo*

30
Statira
Campaspe
sa - ta mi fa-rà guer-ra an - co - ra. In tuo po - ter è l'av-ver-sa - ri - o e puoi ven-di-car sen-za in-du-gio i tor-ti tuo - i. In -
35
cau - ta an-cor non sa - i gli in-gan-ni d'un in - fi - do, nè pro-va-sti il ve - len del dio di Gni-do.
Segue l'aria con violini.

47. Aria

Allegro
Violino I
Violino II
Viola
Campaspe
Continuo
Son men-zo-gne - ri e in - sta - bi - li gli a-man-ti d'og-gi - dì. Son men-zo - gne - ri e in -
5
sta - bi - li, e in-sta - bi - li gli a - man-ti d'og - gi - dì, gli a - man - ti d'og - gi - dì.

10
Dan-no e ri - tol-glio-no a mil - le il cor, e sem-pre vo-glio-no, e sem-pre vo-glio-no can-giar a -
15
mor, con-giar a - mor per-chè sti-man, va-ri - a - bi-li di più go-der co - sì, go-der co-sì, per-chè
20
sti-man, va-ri - a - bi-li, di più go-der co-sì, go-der co - sì.
Son men-zo-gne - ri e in -
Dal segno

Scena v

Statira, Oronte

48. Recitativo

vi - ta e, non so co-me, A-pel-le m'ac-col-se e mi di-fe-se. On-de gra-to il mio cor a lui si re-se m'of-
fer-si a com-pia-cer-lo, e-gli, sa-pen-do che a te ben e-ro no-to, bra-ma che io t'al-lon-ta-ni dall'a-mor d'A-les-san-dro.
Statira
E che gli ca-le?
Oronte
Con no-bi-le de-sir Cam-pa-spe a-do-ra, el-la al tro-no pre-ten-de on-de la mag-gior
cu-ra di que-sto fi-do a-man-te è di ren-der con-ten-to il suo te-so-ro.
Statira
Ci por-ge la for-tu-na un tem-po
giu-sto di se-guir la vir-tù, mol-to all'a-mi-co tu de-vi ed io Cam-pa-spe bra-mo far lie-ta.
Oronte
In-tan-to in-vo-le-rò la te-le
per tron-car o-gni in-du-gio.
Statira
Co-là tra mon-ti al-pe-stri o-ve scor-re l'Eu-fra-te va-do a go-der ro-
mi-ta d'un in-no-cen-te vi-ta, i-vi pre-sto t'at-ten-do e tu sa-ra-i l'u-ni-co mio con-for-to in tan-ti gua-i.

49. Aria

Andante
Statira
Giu-sto nu-me,
giu-sto nu - me que - st'a - ni-ma‿ac - cen - - - - - - de, que-st'a - ni-ma‿ac-
cen - - - - - de di cui fat - to se-gua-ce‿è‿il pen-sier, di cui fat-to to se - gua - - - - - - - - - -
- - - - - - - - - - - - - - - - - - ce, se-gua-ce‿è‿il pen - sier, se - gua-ce‿è‿il pen -
sier. Soscher-ni-re chi tra - di-re la co-stan-za del se-no con - ten-de con l'in-can - - - - - - - - - - -
- - - - - - - - to di mol-le pia-cer, soscher - ni-re chi tra - di-re la co - stan-za del se-no con-ten-de con l'in-
can - to di mol-le pia - cer, di mol-le pia-cer.
Da capo

Ritornello
Violino I
Violino II
Viola
Continuo

30
p
p
p

Scena vi

Oronte solo

50. *Recitativo*

Oronte
Fra le scia-gu - re mi - e pur qual-che mi - te rag - gio go - do d'a-stro be-ni - gno. Mol-to_A-pel - le, ti de - vo
Continuo

30
e se tu sei ca - gio - ne che ve - der pos - sa il mio_a-do - ra - to nu - me, quan-to chiu-do_in me stes - so con -

35
sa - cro al tuo vo - le - re, chè la vi - ta men val, men val, un tal pia - ce - re.

51. Aria

Largo
Oronte
Continuo
Son fe - li - ce fra mar - ti - ri pur - chè mi - ri,
pur - chè mi - ri la ca - gion del - le mie pe - - - - - - - - - - - - - - - - -
ne, del - le mie pe - ne. Cie - co di - o nel mio se - no, nel mio se - no ti de - si - o,
ti de - si - o, strin - gi o - gnor le mie ca - te - - - - - - - - - - - - - - -

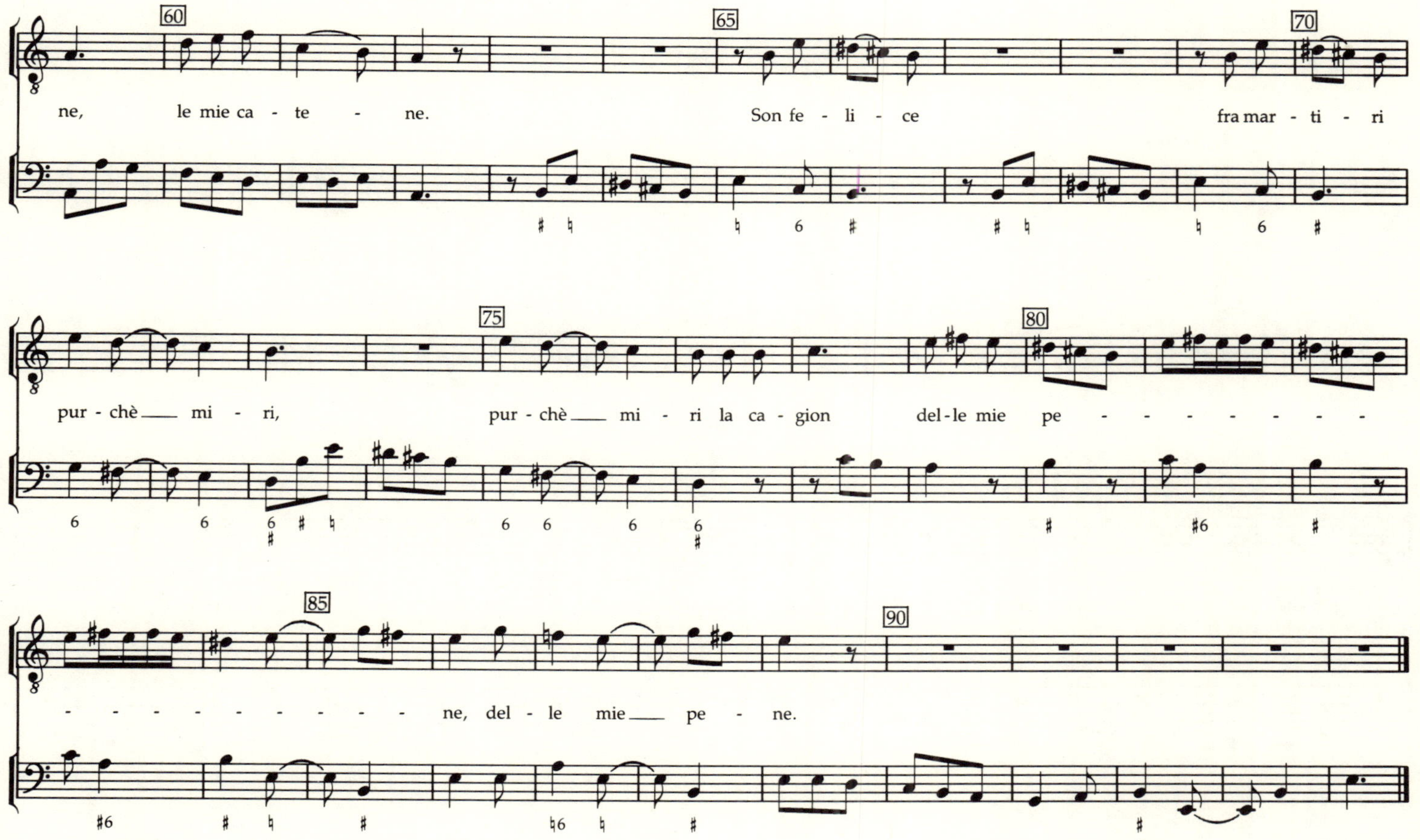

Scena vii

Salone nelle abitazioni di Campaspe con vastissimo carro di fiori nel mezzo e tutto addobbato in guisa della reggia di Flora. Campaspe sopra il carro tirato da due candidissimi corsieri vestita ad imitazione di Flora con il corteggio di molte donzelle che figurano i fiori più cospicui del mondo, e per l'aria quantità d'amorini che spargono al suolo nembi parimenti di fiori.

Alessandro, Apelle, Campaspe

52. *Recitativo*

53. Aria

Andante
Apelle
Continuo
Se t'ap - pa-ga, se t'ap - pa-ga quel sem - bian-te,
per-chè se-co, per-chè se-co u - si ri - gor, per - chè, per - chè, per-chè se - co u - si ri - gor,
u - si ri - gor? Per te so - spi-ra, e so - lo a - spi-ra a go - der - ti in se-no a -
man-te e de - star l'e - stin - to ar - dor. Per te so - spi - ra, e so - lo a - spi - ra a go -
der-ti in se - no a - man-te e de - star l'e - stin - to ar - dor, e de - star l'e - stin - to a - mor.
Da capo
Segue il ritornello.

54. *Aria*

Ritornello
Allegro
Violino I
Violino II
Viola
Campaspe
Continuo
Re - si - - - - - - - - - - - - - sta,

10
re - si - - - - - - - - - - - - - sta, re - si - - - -
15
- - - - - sta, re - si - sta chi può al dar - do d'a - mo - re, al dar -
- - - - - - - - - - - - - - - - do, al dar - do d'a - mo - re, al dar - do d'a - mo - re.

20
Non cu - ra bel - tà chi sen - so non ha,
non cu - ra bel - tà chi sen - so non ha, ma chi la mi - ra le do - na il suo
25
co - re, le do - na il suo co - re, il suo co - re. Re - si
Dal segno

55. *Recitativo*

56. *Aria*

Allegro
Violino I
Violino II
Viola
Campaspe
Continuo
Pu-nir, pu-nir ti vo-glio in-gra - to, in-gra - to, già
so quel che ho da far, quel che ho da far, già so, già so quel che ho da far, quel che ho da far. Le
sma-nie ti dirò che questo sen provò, e se non sei spietato dovrai ben la - gri-mar. Le
p
5
10

57. *Recitativo*

Apelle
lac - cio di me la bra-mi e-ter-na-men - te in brac - cio? Pur-chè re-gni il mio be - ne non ri-cu-so la mor - te, ciò mi det-ta l'af -
Alessandro
fet - to che ho ver - so lei nel pet - to. Il tuo ge - nio sin - ce - ro me - ri - ta, si con - so - li, ti con-se - gno Cam -
Campaspe
Alessandro
pa-spe. Ah, non fia ve-ro! Cam-pa-spe, e tan-to ar-di - sci? Un cor re-gnan-te è gra-zia a-ver a-mi-co e non a-man-te.
Apelle
Ah, non fia ve-ro!

58. Aria

Allegro
Alessandro
Continuo
Chi a vo - lo trop - po al - to dis-pie - ga le
piu - me s'e-spo - ne a ca - der.
Chi a vo - lo trop -
po al - to dis-pie - ga le piu - me s'e-spo - ne a ca - der. Con u - mi-le as - sal-to le stel - le è co -

stu - me, le stel - le è co - stu - me che vin - ca il pen - sier, che vin - ca il pen - sier. Con u - mi - le as - sal - to le stel - le è co -
stu - me, le stel - le è co - stu - me che vin - ca il pen - sier, le stel - le è co - stu - me che vin - ca il pen - sier. Chi a vo - lo trop -
po al - to dis - pie - ga le piu - me s'e - spo - ne a ca - der. Chi a vo - lo trop - po al - to dis - pie - ga le
piu - me s'e - spo - ne a ca - der. Chi a vo - lo trop - po al - to dis - pie - ga le piu - me s'e - spo - ne a ca - der.
Segue il ritornello.
Ritornello
Violino I
Violino II
Viola
Continuo
soli
tutti

Scena viii

Campaspe, Apelle

59. *Recitativo*

60. Aria

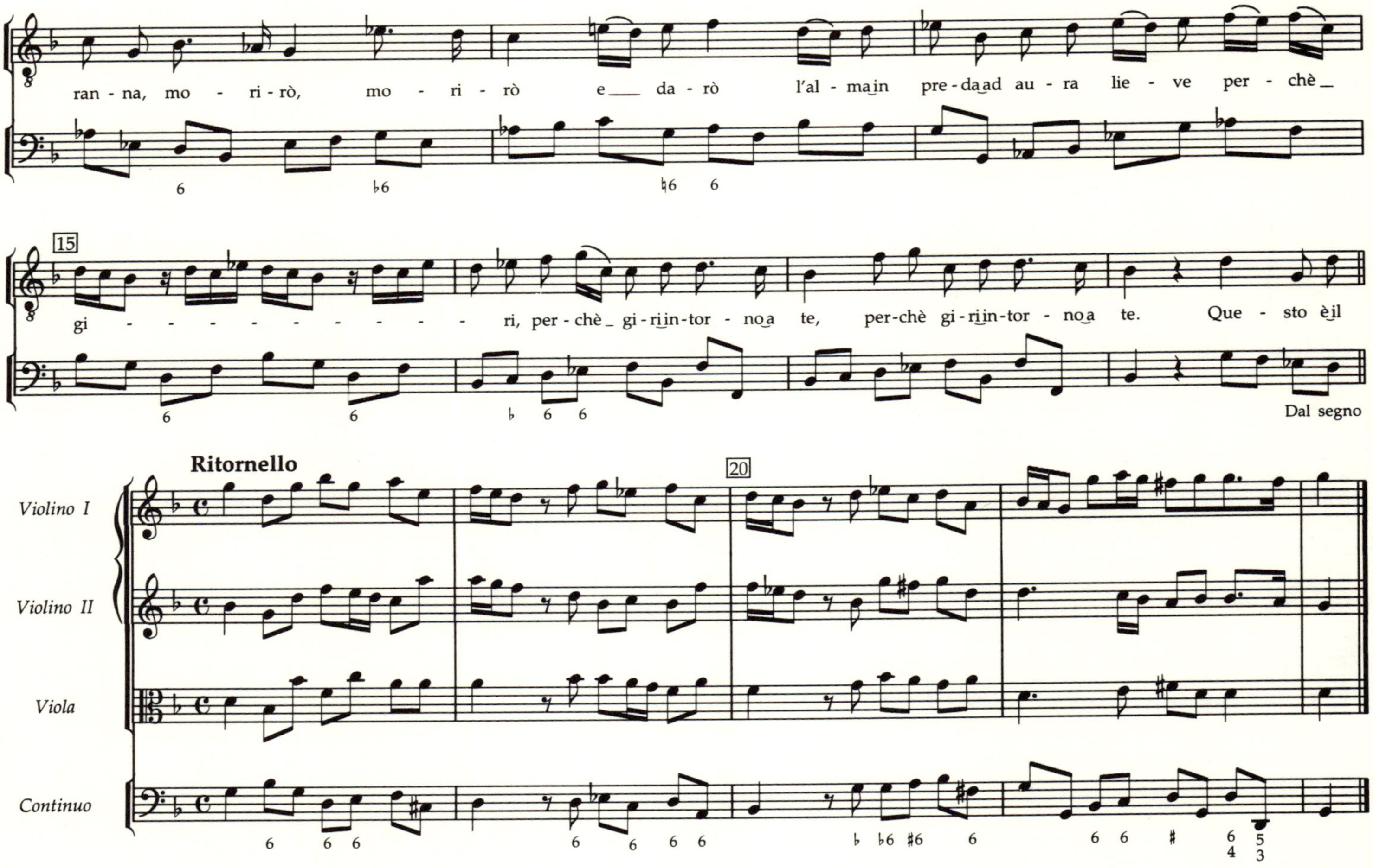

Scena ix

Demetrio, Campaspe, Perinto

61. Recitativo

stra - li, con-tro chi ti sde - gnò sa - ran _ mor - ta - li.
Perinto
Stia-mo‿a sen-tir qual-che biz - zar-ra leg-ge al mi-se-ro De - me - tri - o.
20
Campaspe
Giun-ta‿ap-pe-na Sta - ti - ra a que-sta cor - te, A - les-san-dro di lei va - go si ren - de, la bra-ma per con-sor - te
25
e me dis-pre-gia e‿of - fen-de. Io pian-go e l'as-si - cu - ro del duol che mi tor - men - ta. E - gli‿o-gno-ra più du - ro
30
re - si-ste‿ai miei la - men - ti, e mi con - se - gna spo-sa‿ad A-pel-le.
Demetrio
E non rom-pe-sti il no-do?
Campaspe
Sai pur che re-gia ma - no quan-do‿im-pal-ma due
35
de - stre per di-cre-to fa - tal di que-sto re - gno non si dis-giun-gon più.
Demetrio
Cor - so‿è l'im-pe - gno?
Campaspe
Al - tro che mor-te‿e-gua - le
40
d'A - pel - le e di Sta - ti - ra può scio-glier que-sto lac-cio e te le-var di pe-ne e me d'im-pac-cio. Ri - sol-vi ed e-se-gui - sci.
45
Demetrio
Il bran-do‿im-pu - gno.
Campaspe
Ed io t'at-ten-do, O ca - ro, tut-ta‿ac-ce - sa nel sen di dol-ce a-mo - re, se con-se-gno‿a te so - lo
50
il mio fu - ro - re.
Segue con stromenti.

62. Aria

Allegro
Violino I
Violino II
Viola
Campaspe
Continuo
Sde-gna-to mio co-re, sde-gna-to mio co-re pre-pa-ra-ti all' ar-mi, pre-pa-ra-ti all'
ar-mi, all' ar-
mi, all' ar-mi all' ar-mi.

Voi fu-rie d'A-ver - no u-ni-ti-vi̲a me, u-ni-ti-vi̲a
me, e già che di-scer-no tra-di-ta mia fè, tra-di-ta mia fè, il vo-stro ve-le-no ve-ni-te̲a pre-star-mi,
ve-ni-te, ve-ni-te, ve-ni-te, ve-ni-te̲a pre-star-mi.
Sde-gna-to mio
Dal segno

Scena x

Perinto, Demetrio

63. Recitativo

64. Aria

15
re. In-se-gna-te-mi, mo-stra-te-mi il ve-len, il ve-len che ce-la-te nel sen, se per se-guir a-
20
mor ar-mar-si di fu-ror, ar-mar-si di fu-
ror de-ve il pen-sie-re, ar-mar-si del fu-ror
25
de-ve il pen-sie-re.
30
A voi di-man-do il cor, a voi di-man-do il
35
cor, di-man-do il cor bel-ve più fie-re, bel-ve più fie-
40
re.

Scena xi

Statira, che esce dalla sua picciola grotta.

65. *Recitativo*

Segue l'aria con due violini.

66. Aria

Largo
Violino I
Violino II
Statira
Continuo
Quei so - spir,
quei so - spir che spar - si al ven - - - - - - - - - - - - - -
- - - - - - - - - - - - - - - - - - to
fat - ta gra - ve han l'a - ria in -

30
tor - no, fat - ta gra - ve han
35
40
l'a - - - - - - - - - - ria — in - tor - no, han l'a - - - - - - - - - - ria — in - tor -
45
50
no. Pren-dan for - ma dal — tor - men - to

55
ed a me fac - cian _ ri - tor -
60
65
no. Pren - dan for - ma dal ___ tor - men - - - - - - - - - - - - - - - - -
70
75
- - to ed ___ a me fac - cian ri - tor - - no, fac - - - cian ri - tor - - - no.
Da capo

67. *Recitativo*

68. Ritornello

A questo suono, Statira appoggiata ad un sasso s'addormenta.

Scena xii

Demetrio, e Statira che dorme

69. *Recitativo*

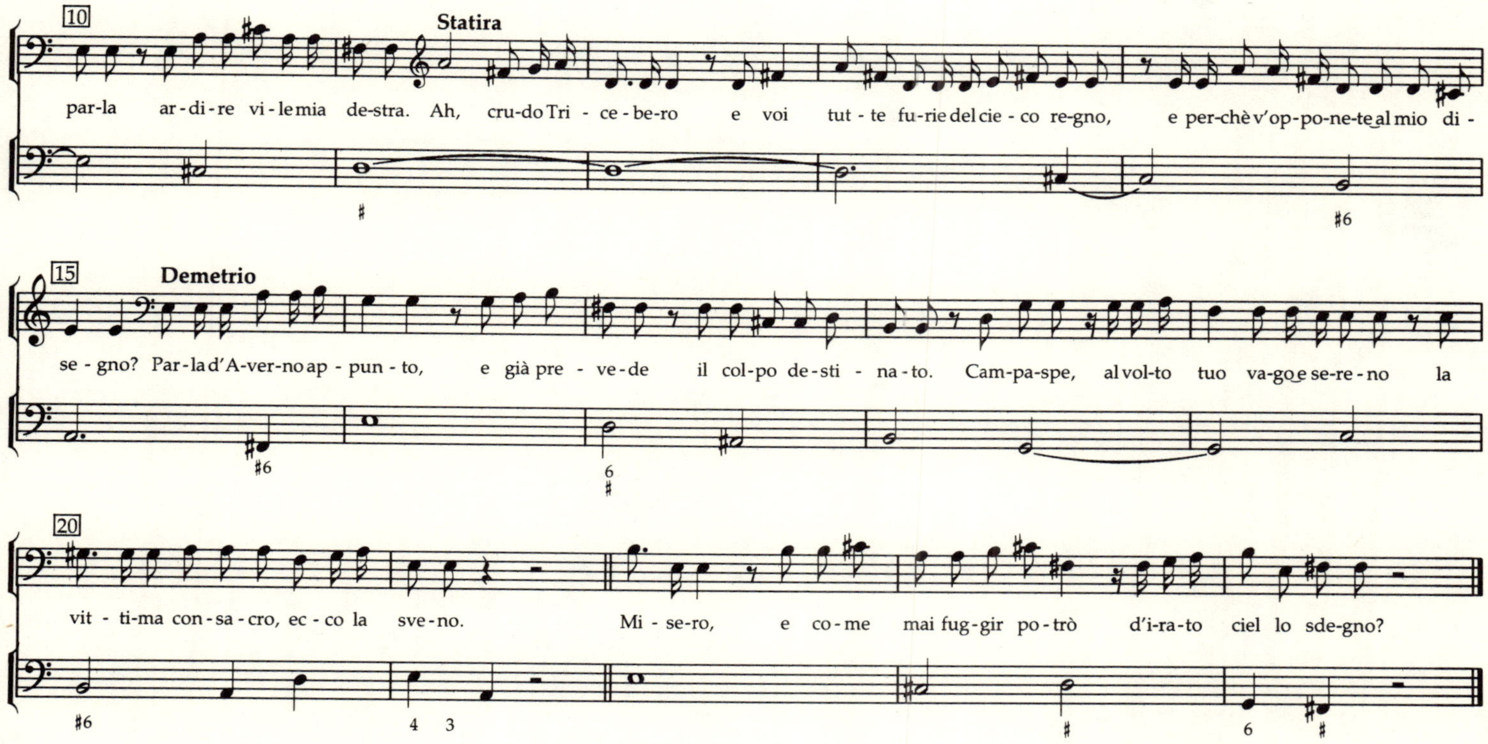

Fugge Demetrio, e con fulmini, lampi, e tuoni segue fierissimo terremoto.

ATTO TERZO

Scena i

Alessandro solo

70. *Aria*

20
te - re il mio cor, chè ful - mi - ne non ha - i, chè ful - mi - ne non ha - i d'ab - bat - te -
Andante
solo
tutti
25
re il mio cor. Ti - ran - no, ti - ran - no, e che pre - ten - di
do - mar quest' al - ma an - cor, do - mar quest' al - ma an - cor.

71. *Recitativo*

72. Aria

Scena ii

Apelle solo

73. Aria

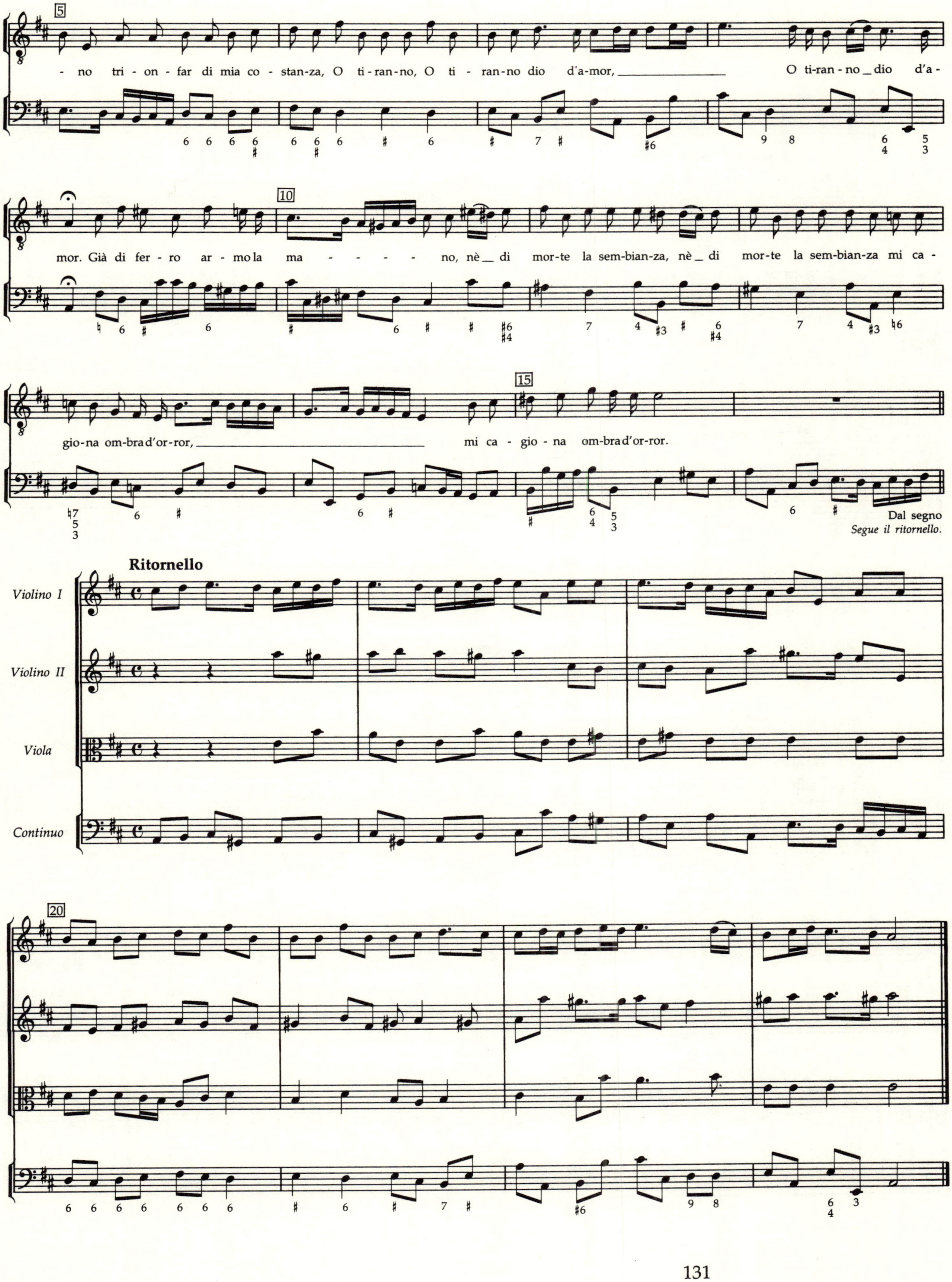
5
- no tri - on - far di mia co - stan-za, O ti-ran-no, O ti - ran-no dio d'a-mor, O ti-ran - no _ dio d'a -
10
mor. Già di fer - ro ar - mo la ma - - - - no, nè _ di mor-te la sem-bian-za, nè _ di mor-te la sem-bian-za mi ca -
15
gio-na ombra d'or-ror, mi ca - gio - na om-bra d'or-ror.
Dal segno
Segue il ritornello.
Ritornello
Violino I
Violino II
Viola
Continuo
20

74. *Recitativo*

Apelle
Continuo
A-mai Cam-pa-spe e l'a-mo. Nè d'al-tro fo-co ac-ce-so e-ra il mio fi-do se-no che di quel va-go
lu-me con cui vir-tù le da-va for-za e le-na. Ma giac-chè vuol co-sì, giac-chè vuol la mia pe-na il ciel, il
mon-do, e l'i-do-lo che a-do-ro, del ciel, del mon-do, e del mio ben l'im-pe-ro e-se-gui-sca ver me col-po se-ve-ro.

Vuol uccidersi e vien trattenuto da Oronte.

Scena iii

Oronte, Apelle, voce di dentro di Campaspe

75. *Recitativo*

Oronte
Apelle
Continuo
A-mi-co, e qual scia-gu-ra ti gui-da a sì gran duo-lo? Ob-be-dir mi con-vie-ne. A chi? Al de-sti-no. Ta-lor il
sag-gio al fa-to por-ge re-go-la. È ve-ro, ma non sen-te ra-gio-ni un dis-pe-ra-to, la-scia-mi. Che pre-ten-di? Ter-mi-nar le scia-
gu-re. Deh, ri-tor-na in te stes-so. Al-tro non fai che pro-lon-gar-mi il duo-lo. Il tem-po dà con-si-glio. La for-tu-na mi sprez-za.

Scena iv

Campaspe difendendosi dalle zanne d'un leone quale viene ucciso da Oronte e da Apelle.

Apelle, Campaspe, Oronte

76. *Recitativo*

Segue l'aria con violini.

77. Aria

A tempo giusto
Violino I
Violino II
Viola
Campaspe
Continuo
T'of - fe - si, t'of - fe - si ben mi - o, or chie - do, chie - do pie - ta, ben mi - o, ben
mi - o, or chie - do, _ chie - do pie - tà, pie - tà, pie - tà, or chie - do, _ chie - do pie -
tà, or chie - do, _chie-do pie - tà. Qual fui più non so - no, qual fui più non so - no, ma cer-co il per-do-no, cer-co il per -
p
solo
5
10

78. *Recitativo*

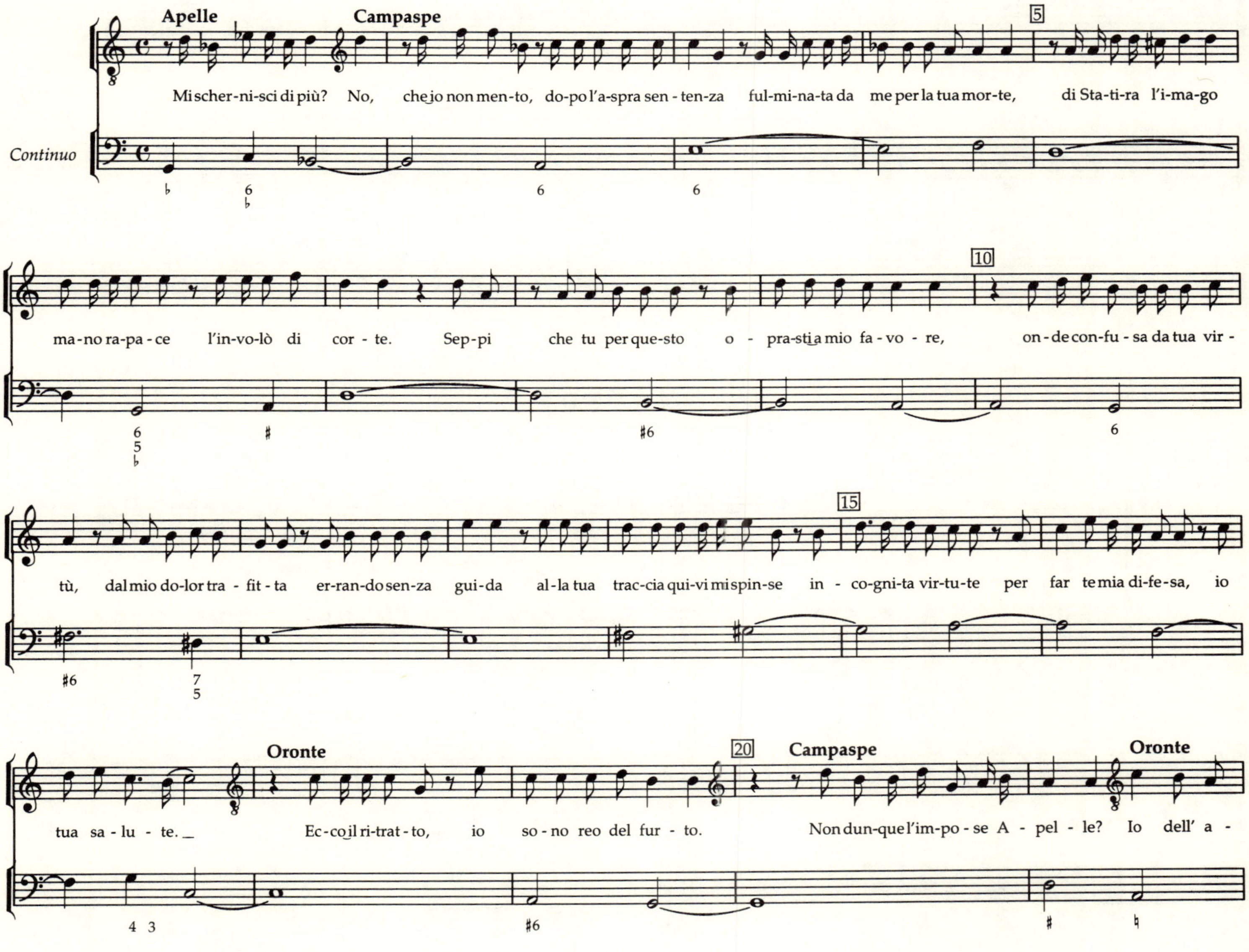

Campaspe
mi-co at-ten-to a so-dis - far le vo-glie, ed av-ver-sa Sta - ti - ra a-gli a-mo-ri del re, con sen-so e-gua-le fu ra-pi-ta la te-la. E
pu - re so - no quell' in-gra - ta, quell' em - pia che la vi - ta d'A - pel - le e di Sta-ti - ra o-diai co - tan - to? In gra - ve
ri-schio di mor-te gia-ce per mia col-pa l'in-no-cen - te stra - nie - ra. El-vio, spe - di - to muo-vi ver lei le pian-te ad im-pe-dir l'ec-ces-so.
Oronte
Oh dei, che sen - to? Per di-fen-der Sta-ti - ra i van-ni al pie - de, tol-ti al fian - co d'a-mor, mi dà la fe - de.

79. Aria

Assai spiritosa
Oronte
Continuo
Deh, so - spen - - - di
il fer - ro a - cu - to Clo - to fie - ra a sì bel sta - me, a sì bel

15
sta - - - - - - - - - - me, a sì bel sta - - - - - - - - - - me.
20
E ri - vol - gi a crin ca - nu - to
25
i tuoi sde - gni e le tue bra - me.
E ri - vol - - - - - - - - - - - - gi a crin ca - nu - to i tuoi
30
35
sde - gni e le tue bra - me, i tuoi sde - gni e le tue bra - me.
40
Dal segno
Segue il ritornello.
Ritornello
45
50
Violino I
Violino II
Viola
Continuo

Seconda stanza
55
Campaspe
Continuo
Non ten - tar in -
60
65
giu - sto fa - to di ra - pir sì va - go fio - re, sì va - go
70
fio - - - - - - - - - - - re, sì va - go fio - - - - - - - - - - re.
75
E con ci - bo me - no gra - to a - li - men - ta il tuo fu - ro -
80
85
re. E con ci - - - - - - - - - - - - - - bo me - no gra - to a - li -
90
men - ta il tuo fu - ro - re, a - li - men - ta il tuo fu - ro - re.
Dal segno

Scena v

Apelle, Campaspe

80. *Recitativo*

81. Aria

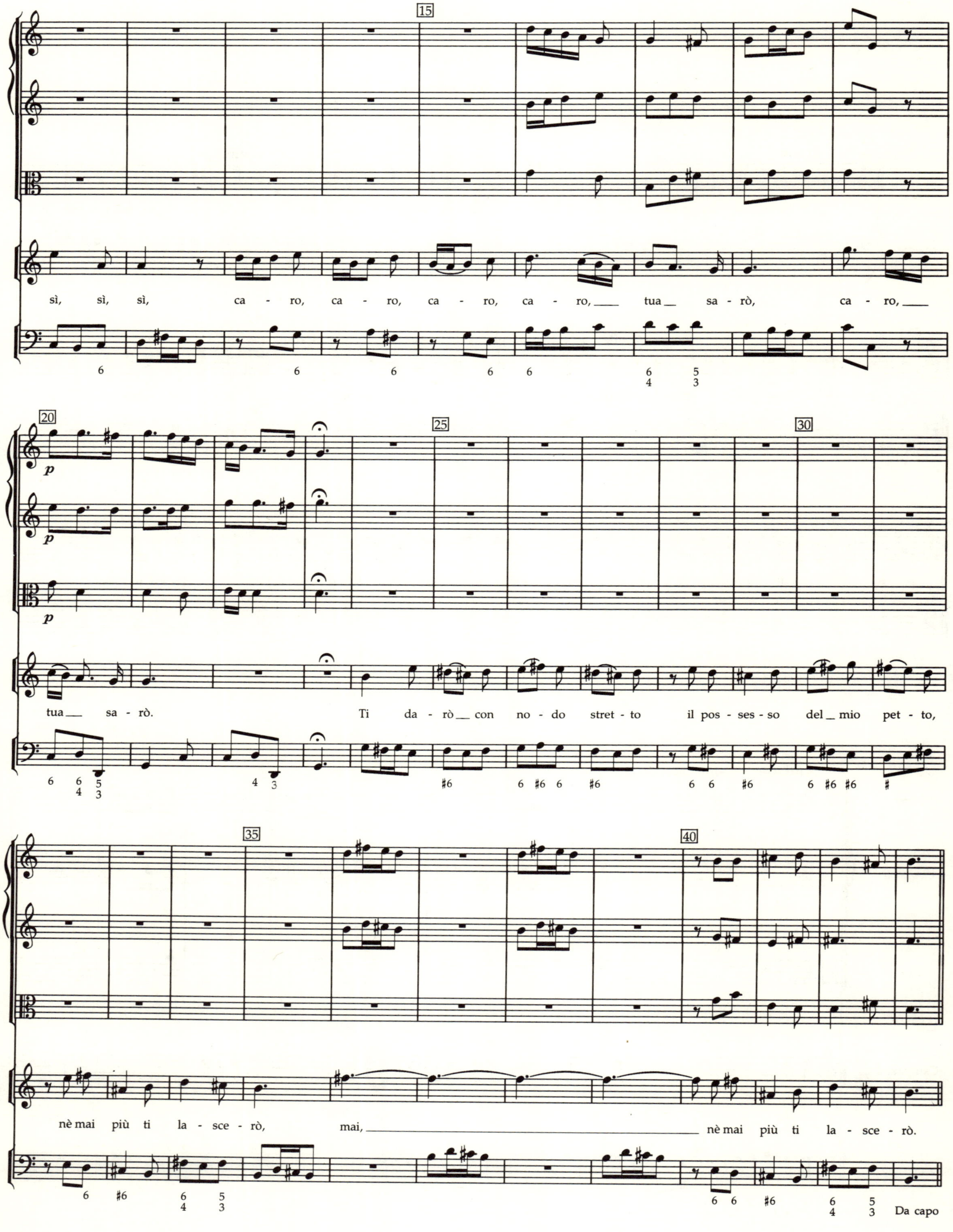
15
sì, sì, sì, ca - ro, ca - ro, ca - ro, ca - ro, tua sa - rò, ca - ro,
20
25
30
p
tua sa - rò. Ti da - rò con no - do stret - to il pos - ses - so del mio pet - to,
35
40
nè mai più ti la - sce - rò, mai, nè mai più ti la - sce - rò.
Da capo

82. *Arietta*

Andante
Apelle
La-scia-mi, la-scia-mi che al-la mor-te il ciel mi de-sti-nò, il ciel mi de-sti-nò, il ciel mi de-sti-
nò. Nè ai vez-zi del-la sor-te più ce-de-re non vo', più ce-de-re non vo'. La-scia-mi,
la-scia-mi, che al-la mor-te, il ciel mi de-sti-nò, il ciel mi de-sti-nò, il ciel mi de-sti-nò.
5
10

83. *Recitativo*

Campaspe
Apelle
Continuo
Vi-vi, e vi-vi per me, dol-ce a-mor mi-o. D'ob-be-dir-ti il de-si-o sem-pre for-za mag-
gio-re pren-de in que-sto mio co-re. Ec-co-mi, e mor-to e vi-vo a tuo pia-ce-re, chè mia vi-ta e mia
mor-te, chè mia vi-ta e mia mor-te è il tuo vo-le-re.
5
10
15

Segue Apelle l'aria con violini.

84. Aria

Andante et amoroso
Violino I
Violino II
Viola
Apelle
Continuo
Sì, sì, bel - la, bel - la, vie - ni a me, bel - la,
vie - ni, sì, sì, sì, bel - la, bel - la, bel - la, bel - la,
vie - ni a me, bel - la, vie - ni a me.
E com -

25
30
pen - sa a tan - te pe - ne col do - nar a me quel be - ne per cui giu - ro e - ter - na
35
40
fè, e - ter - - - - - - - - - - - - - na, per cui giu - ro e - ter - na fè.
Da capo

85. Recitativo

Campaspe
Apelle
Campaspe
Continuo
Van-ne, O cru-del, chè io non ho cor per te. Ca - ra, ca - ra non più. Le fiam - me che a fa-vor d'A-les -
5
Apelle
san - dro ten - ta - sti su - sci - tar in que - sto se - no ri - sen - to in que - sto pun - to. Deh, por - gi ter - mi - ne al - le mie
10
pe - ne, a - ni - ma mi - a, e in que - sto pet - to o - gni do - lor ob - li - a.
Segue a 2.

86. *Duetto*

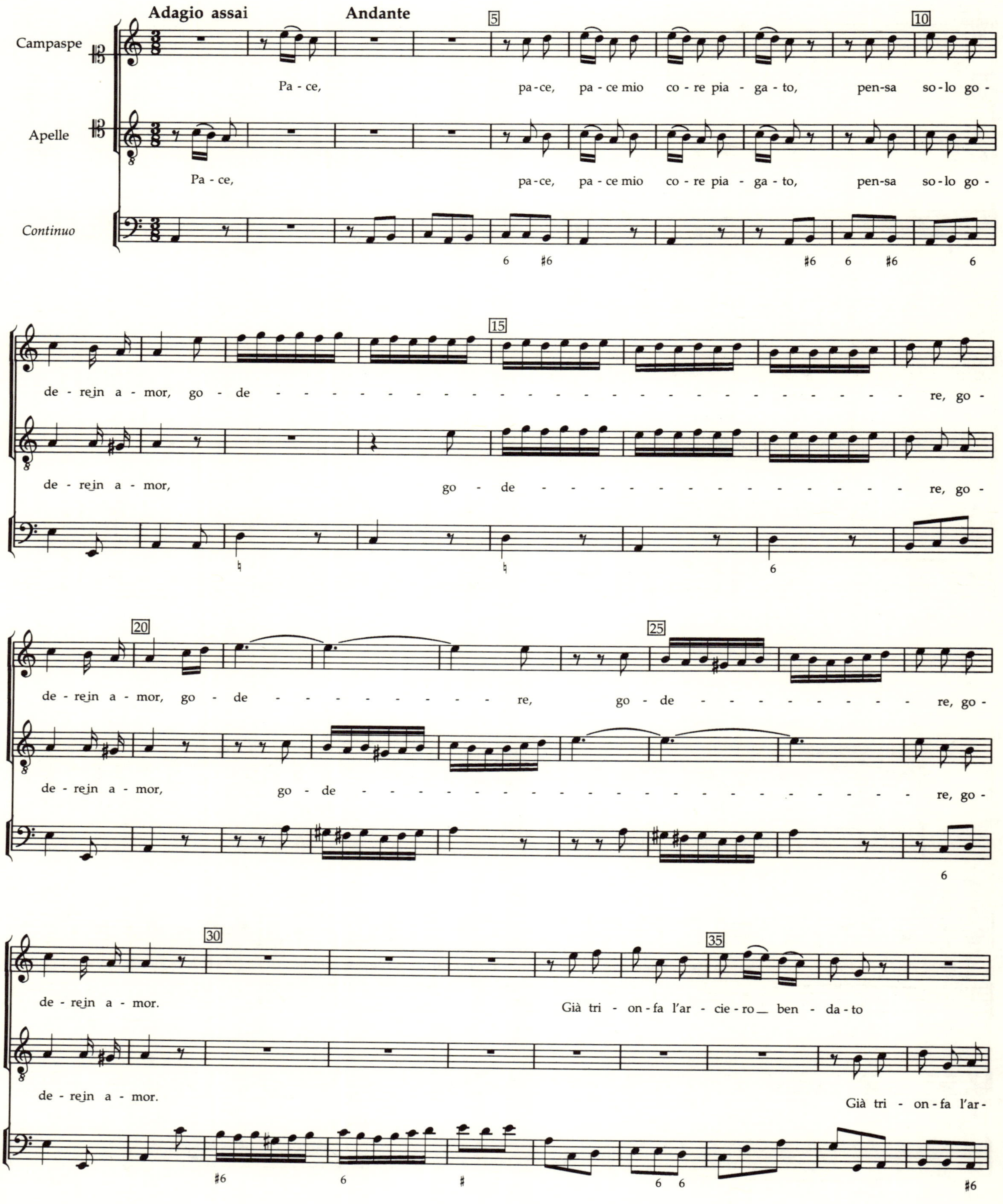
Adagio assai
Andante
Campaspe
Apelle
Continuo
Pa - ce, pa - ce, pa - ce mio co - re pia - ga - to, pen - sa so - lo go -
Pa - ce, pa - ce, pa - ce mio co - re pia - ga - to, pen - sa so - lo go -
de - re_in a - mor, go - de - - - re, go -
de - re_in a - mor, go - de - - - re, go -
de - re_in a - mor, go - de - - - re, go - de - - - re, go -
de - re_in a - mor, go - de - - - re, go -
de - re_in a - mor. Già tri - on - fa l'ar - cie - ro ben - da - to
de - re_in a - mor. Già tri - on - fa l'ar -

40
45
e sen fug - ge dal pet - to il ri - gor,
cie - ro ben - da - to e sen fug - ge dal pet - to il ri - gor, e
e sen fug - ge dal pet - to il ri - gor.
sen fug - ge dal pet - to il ri - gor.
50
Adagio
Andante
55
Pa - ce, pa - ce,
60
pa - ce mio co - re pia - ga - to, pen - sa so - lo go - de - re in a - mor, go - de
go -
65
70
re, go - de - re in a - mor, go - de
de re, go - de - re in a - mor, go - de
75
80
re, go - de re go - de - re in a - mor, go - de - re in a - mor.
re, go - de - re in a - mor, go - de - re in a - mor.

Scena vi

Bosco che discende dall'eremo di Statira in una valle.
Perinto con soldati

87. *Recitativo*

Perinto
Il ge-lo - so re-gnan-te con bel pre - te - sto a cu - sto - dir in - vi - a la sua va - ga Sta - ti - ra, non già per-chè pa -
Continuo
6
4 3

5
ven - ti d'in - si - di - o - so ag - gua - to al suo bel nu - me, so - lo per-chè de - vo - ti al - tri se - gua - ci non le por - gan vo - ti.
6
4 3

10
Ma se sa-pes - se po - i a qual op - ra cru - del De-me-trio a-spi - ra, al - lo - ra sì che guar - de - ria Sta - ti - ra.
#6
4 3

Segue Perinto l'aria con violini.

88. Aria

Allegro
Violino I
Violino II
Viola
Perinto
Continuo
5
Non v'è ri - me - di - o, non v'e ri - me - di - o, chi se-gue a - mo - re non ha mai
6 6
6 6
6
6 6 #6
4 3

10
ben, non_ha mai ben, chi se-gue_a - mo - re, chi se-gue_a - mo - re non ha mai ben, non ha mai
15
ben. Ge - lo - so te - di - o to - glie dal co - re o - gni se -
20
ren. Ge - lo - so te - di - o to - glie dal co - re o - gni se - ren. Non v'è ri - me - di - o,
Dal segno

Scena vii

Statira appoggiata al braccio d'Oronte
scende il monte del bosco.

Statira, Oronte, Perinto da parte

89. *Recitativo*

Statira
Oronte
Nul - la pos-so ca-pir. Som-mo pe - ri-glio di vi-o-len-te fa - to sov-ra-star al tuo ca-po mi con-fes-sò Cam - pa-spe.
5
Statira
E chi lo
Continuo
Oronte
Perinto
Statira
10
ten - ta? Que-sto non m'è pa - le - se. Lo so ben io chè son qui del pa-e - se. Il ciel rav-ve-da il co-re dell' em-pio tra-di -
15
to - re. E tu, Pren-ci-pe O - ron - te, se an-cor il re - o di ri - tro-var t'è da - to o-blia lo sde-gno, e ce-di la ven -
Perinto
Oronte
20
det - ta al To-nan-te del Cie-lo a cui s'a-spet-ta. In-au-di-ta pie-tà. Som-ma cle - men-za. Ma Si - gno-ra, che gen-te in
Statira
Perinto
25
bel-li-co-sa for-ma cu-sto - di-sco-no il bo - sco? O - là, qual gui-da qui-vi vi por-ta a-mi-ci? Per ren-der più si-cu-ra il
Statira
30
Perinto
Re la tua di-mo-ra, que-sti ar - cie-ri t'in-vi - a. Trop-po, trop-po m'o - no - ra. Van-ne al Re, dì che se-co bra-mo di fa-vel - lar. Par-to ve-lo - ce.

Scena viii

Statira, Oronte, e poi Demetrio

90. *Recitativo*

Statira
Oronte
Statira
Continuo
An-cor, Pren-ce, ri - flet-to al tuo di-scor - so.
È cer-to.
Ma qual col-pa Cam-pa-spe ve-de in me de-gna di mor - te?
Oronte
Ge-lo-sia d'A-les-san - dro un dì la spin-se, ed or pian-ge il suo fal - lo.
Statira
I - gno-to al mon-do sa-rà dun-que per sem - pre l'uc-ci-sor di Sta-ti - ra?
Demetrio
Io non m'a-scon-do al - le giu-ste i-re tu - e, Re-al Si-gno-ra, ec-co-ti l'i-ni - mi - co, l'uc-ci-sor di Sta-ti-ra, quel-la fu-ri-a, quel mo-stro al cui bar-ba-ro ar - di-re crol-lò il cie-lo, la ter-ra, e il fo-sco re-gno. Sì quell' io son d'o-gni pie-ta-de in-de-gno.

Segue Demetrio l'aria con violini.

91. Aria

Grave
Violino I
Violino II
Viola
Demetrio
Continuo
Gran ci-men-to, gran ci-men-to al tuo gran

5
co - re, al tuo gran co - re ti ca - gio-na il mio fal-lir, il mio fal - lir, il mio fal-lir, ti ca - gio-na il mio fal-lir.
10
La cle - men-za ed il ri - go - re lo vor - reb - be-ro, lo vor-reb - be - ro ra - pir. La cle-men-za ed il ri -
6 5
4 3
15
go - re lo vor-reb - be-ro, lo vor - reb - be - ro ra - pir, lo vor-reb - be - ro ra - pir.
Dal segno

92. *Recitativo*

Segue subito l'aria con violini.

93. Aria

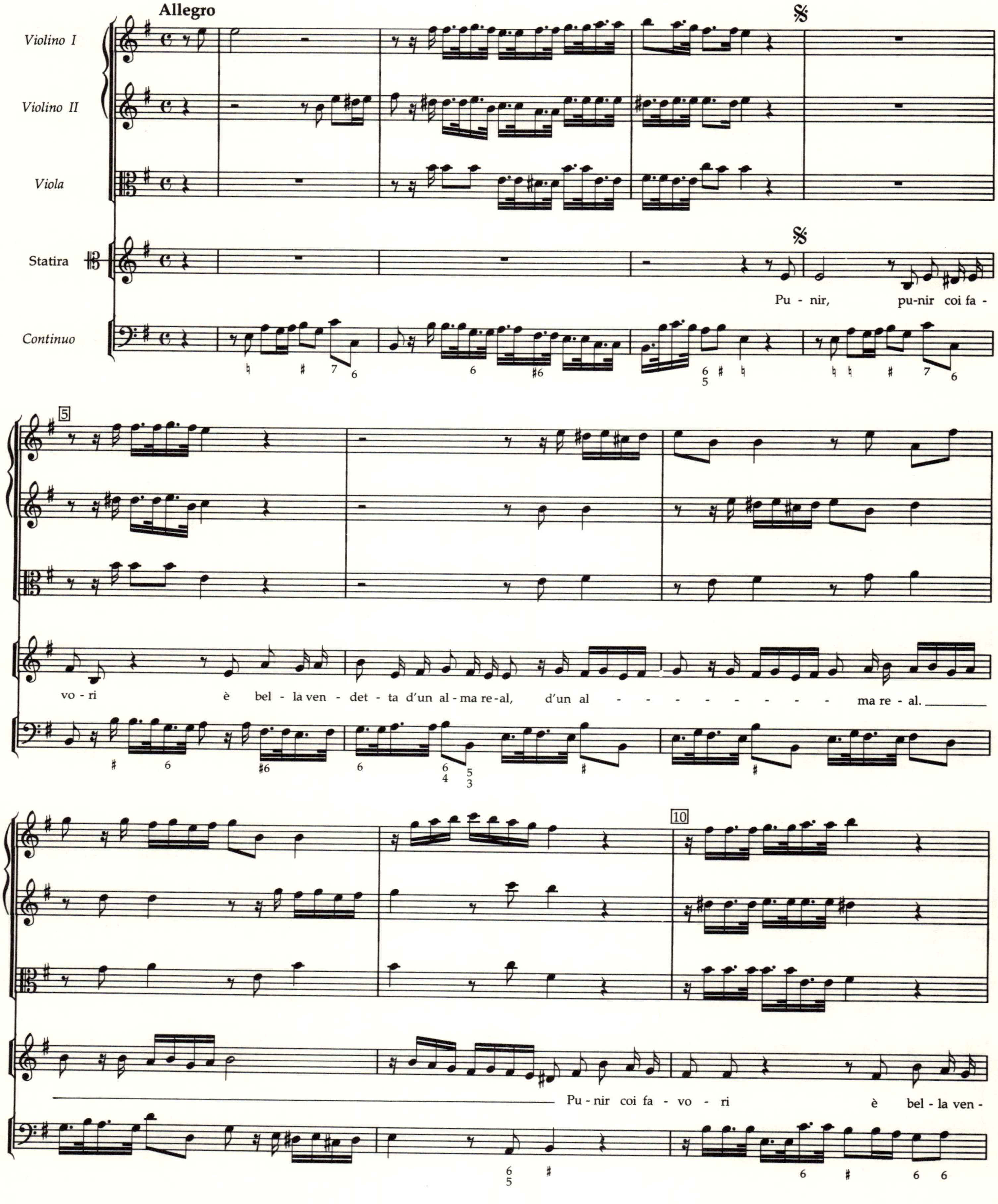
Allegro
Violino I
Violino II
Viola
Statira
Continuo
Pu - nir, pu-nir coi fa -
vo - ri è bel - la ven - det - ta d'un al - ma re - al, d'un al - - - - - - - - - ma re - al.
Pu - nir coi fa - vo - ri è bel - la ven -

det-ta d'un al-ma re-al, d'un al-ma re-al. Per vin-ce-re i co-ri, per vin-ce-re i co-ri sì dol-ce sa-
15
et-ta o-gni al-tra pre-val, o-gni al-tra pre-
20
val. Per vin-ce-re i co-ri sì dol-ce sa-et-ta o-gni al-tra pre-val. Pu-
Dal segno

Scena ix

Gran piazza con archi trionfali e palazzo regio in prospettiva con portone aperto custodito da guardie e popolo numeroso sopra le finestre.

Alessandro, Apelle

94. *Recitativo*

95. Aria

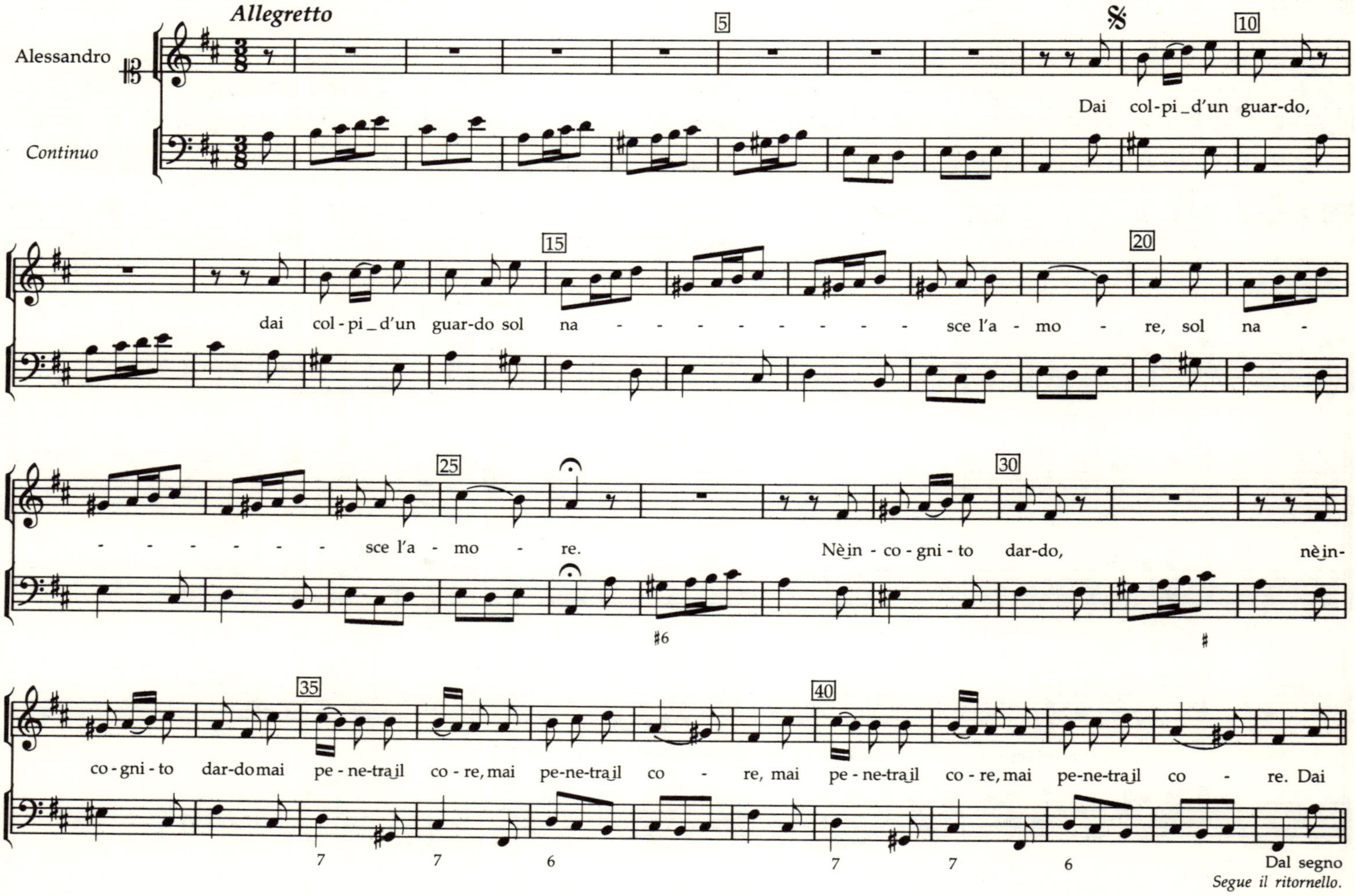

Ritornello
Violino I
Violino II
Viola
Continuo
45
50
55
p
Seconda stanza
Alessandro
Continuo
60
65
Chi por-ta_nel pet-to,
70
75
chi por-ta_nel pet-to d'a-mo - - - - - - - - - re la pia - ga, d'a-mo - - - - - - - - re la pia - ga.
80
85
90
Per dar-le-ri-cet-to, per dar-le_ri-cet-to la vid-de es-ser va-ga, la vid-de es-ser va - ga, la vid-de es-ser va-ga, la vid-de es-ser va - ga. Chi
95
100
Dal segno

96. *Recitativo*

97. Aria

Andante
Violino I
Violino II
Viola
Apelle
Continuo
Va - go, va - go rag - gio di __ spe - ran - - za,
va - go, va - go rag - gio di __ spe - ran - za dà __ sem - bian - za di __ con - ten - to, dà __ sem - bian - za di __ con - ten - to al mio do -
lor, al mio do - lor, dà __ sem -

bian - za di __ con - ten - to al mio do - lor. Son gio - ie le pe - ne ed han per - so o - gni _ ri - gor le __ ca -
15
te - ne che __ mi por - ge il cie - co a - mor. Son gio - ie le pe - ne ed __ han per - so o - gni ri -
20
gor le ca - te - ne che mi por - ge il cie - co a - mor, il cie - co a - mor, il cie - co a - mor. Va - go, va - go rag - gio di __ spe -
Dal segno

Scena x

Perinto correndo, Alessandro

98. *Recitativo*

Perinto
Si - gnor, Si - gnor, vi - ci - na è già la prin - ci - pes - sa, ec - co ve - lo - ci la pre -
Continuo
4 3
Alessandro
5
Perinto
cor - ro - no i ser - vi. Al tem - pio in - via Sta - ti - ra o - ve l'at - ten - do. Ub - bi - di - rò (t'in - ten - do).

99. Aria

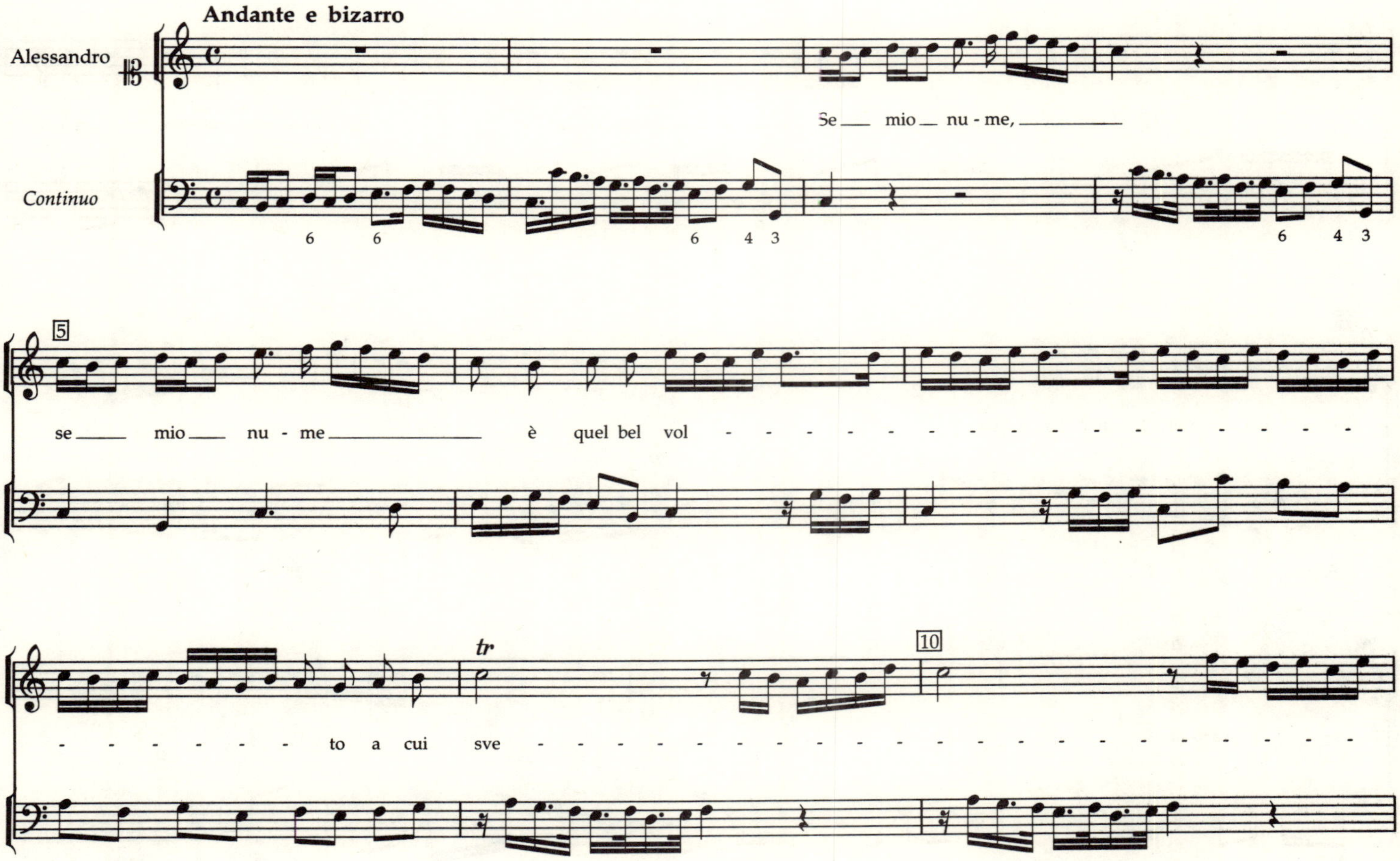
Andante e bizarro
Alessandro
Continuo
Se mio nu - me,
6 6
6 4 3
6 4 3
5
se mio nu - me è quel bel vol - to a cui sve -
tr
10

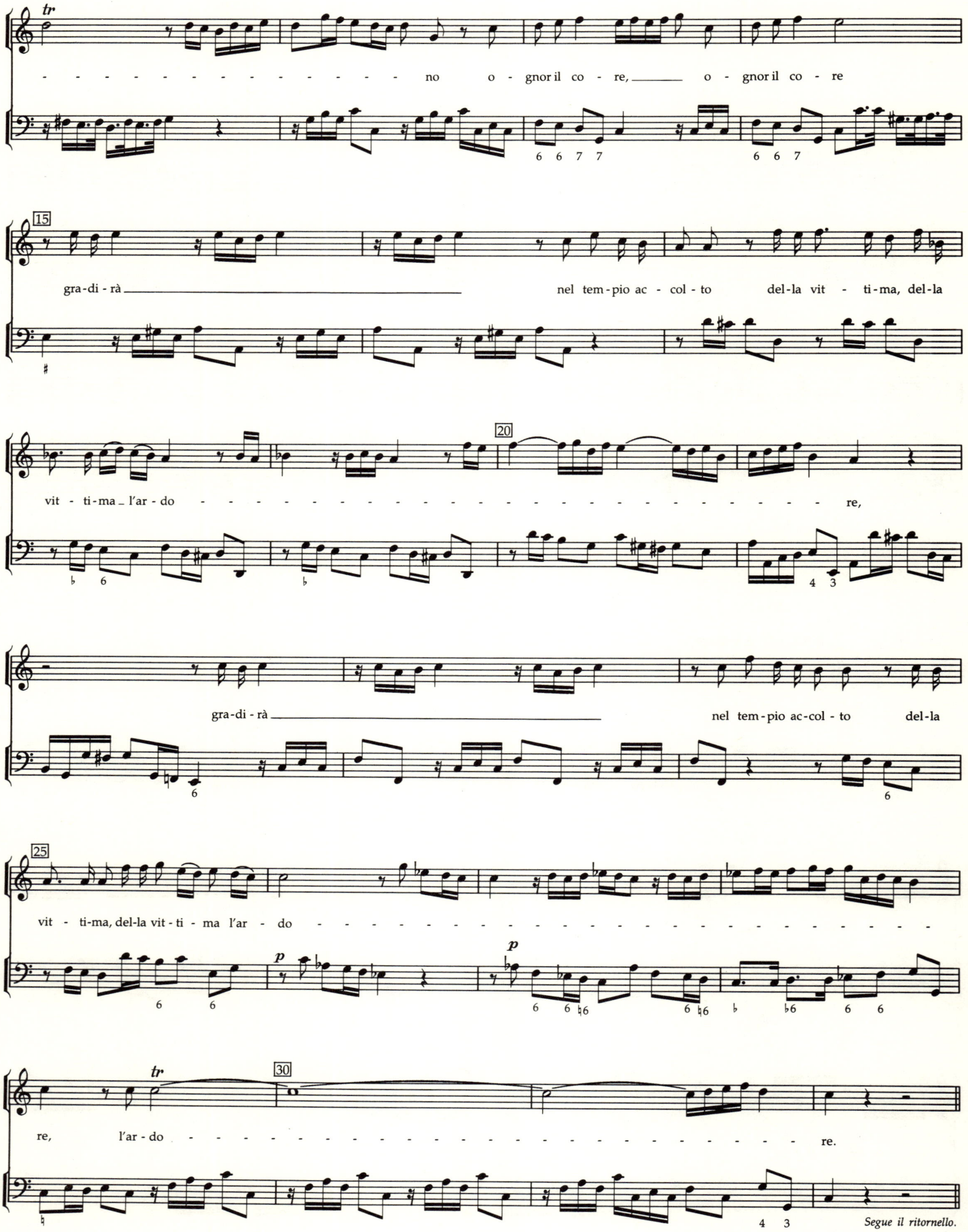

tr
- - - - - - - - - - - - - - - - no o - gnor il co - re, o - gnor il co - re
15
gra-di-rà nel tem-pio ac-col-to del-la vit - ti-ma, del-la
20
vit - ti-ma l'ar-do - re,
gra-di-rà nel tem-pio ac-col-to del-la
25
vit - ti-ma, del-la vit-ti - ma l'ar - do -
p
p
30
re, l'ar-do - re.
Segue il ritornello.

Scena xi

Perinto, Campaspe

100. *Recitativo*

5
Perinto
Sol d'A-pel-le la fe-de gra-di-sco. Sag-gia-men-te, quel che a-ver non po - te-te mo-stra-te dis-prez - zar mo-de-sta-men - te.
4 3
6 5 ♯ ♯
Campaspe
10
Perinto
Campaspe
Ma, De-me-tri-o? De - te-sto. Pur di lui vi ser - vi-te per bra-vo nei bi - so-gni. Un mez-zo in - giu-sto, quan-do sem-bra che
♯
15
Perinto
gui-di al por-to a-ma - to, i se-gua-ci de-lu-de e ser-ve al fa-to. Ma cre-sce o-gnor la cal - ca. Al tem-pio, al tem-pio in-driz-
4 3
20
Campaspe
za - te-vi a-mi - ci, co - là v'at-ten-de il re. Bra-mo al-le pian-te anch' i - o di Sta-ti - ra la bel - la
♯
Perinto
25
pian-ger il fal-lo mi - o. Di cor dol-ce e be-ni - gno la tro-ve-rai, più av-vez-za a gra - dir le pre-ghie-re che a pu -
♯6
Campaspe
Perinto
Campaspe
Perinto
30
Campaspe
ni-re gli er-ro-ri. Dun-que pos-so spe-rar? Più che non bra-mi. Ver lei m'in-vi-o. Non du-bi-tar. Con-fi-do.
♯ 4 3 ♯ 43 ♯ ♯6 6 4 3

Scena xii

Corteggiata da paggi, alabardieri, moschettieri e moltitudine di servitori, vi si vede Statira dentro bellisima lettiga scoperta, la quale, fermata nel mezzo della scena, smonta appoggiata da Oronte.

Statira, Perinto, Campaspe, Oronte

101. *Recitativo*

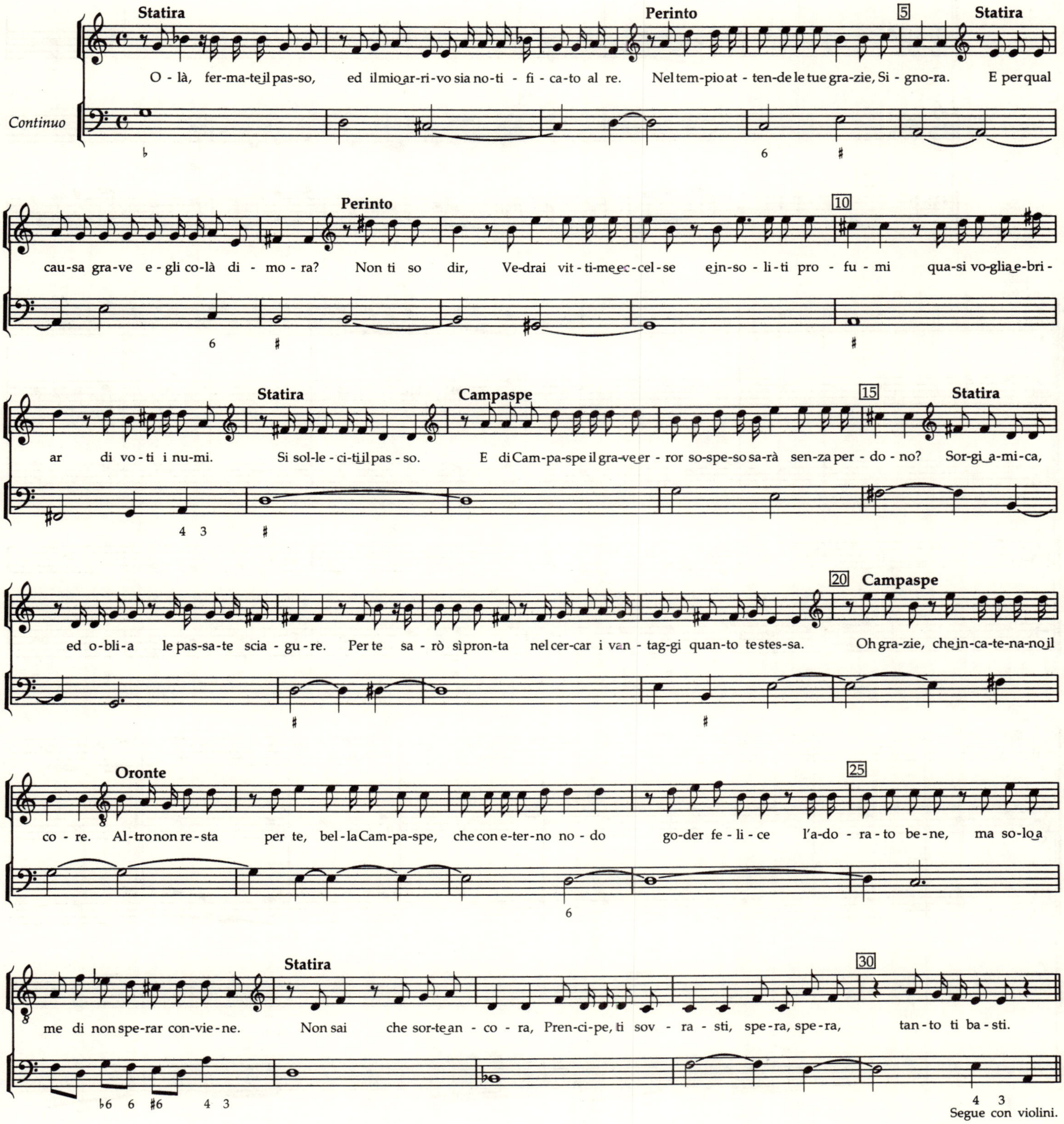

102. Aria

Amoroso
Violino I
Violino II
Viola
Statira
Continuo
Dei tuoi_do - lo - ri por - to nel se - no,
por - to nel se - no pe - gno co - stan - ti, por - to nel se - no
pe - gno co - stan - te, co - stan te, pe - gno co - stan - te co - stan - -

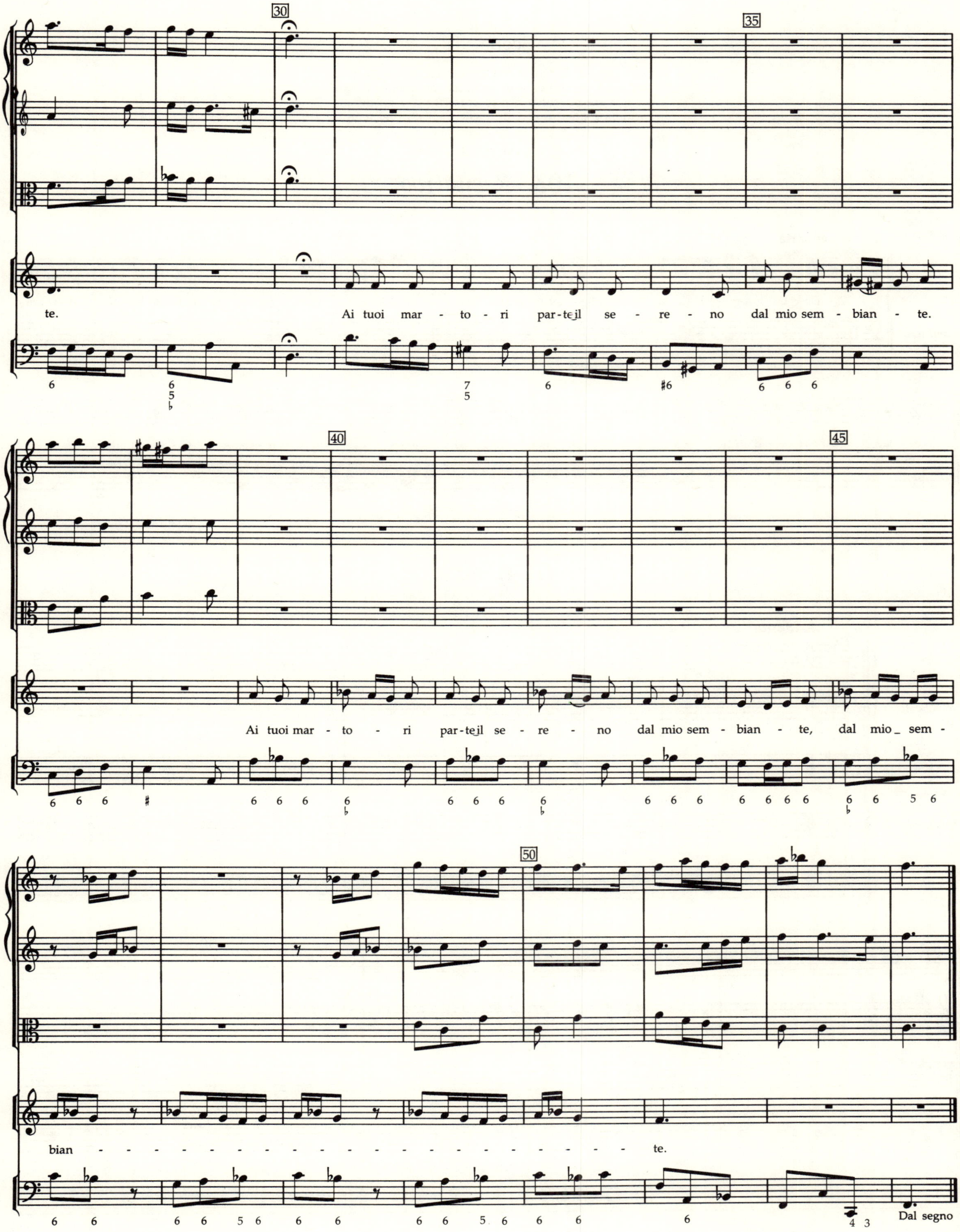
30
35
te.
Ai tuoi mar - to - ri par - te il se - re - no dal mio sem - bian - te.
40
45
Ai tuoi mar - to - ri par - te il se - re - no dal mio sem - bian - te, dal mio sem -
50
bian - te.
Dal segno

Scena xiii

Tempio di Diana con altare preparato per il
sacrificio, moltitudine di sacerdoti nel mezzo ai quali
vi sta un cervo bianco coronato di rose per
vittima e quattro cori di musici nell'alto del tempio.

Demetrio solo

103. *Recitativo*

Demetrio
Da che lun-gi a-gli a-mo-ri vol-go sciol-te le pian-te con in-so-li-ta pa-ce go-do di li-ber-tà l'au-ra gra-
Continuo
5
di-ta, se il vi-ver d'un a-man-te è mo-rir ad o-gnor, re-stan-do in vi-ta.

Segue Demetrio l'aria con violini.

104. Aria

Andante
Violino I
Violino II
Viola
Demetrio
Continuo
5
10
Ca - sta De - - - - -

15
- - a, Ca - sta De - - - - - - - - a, fo
20
vo - - - - - - - - - to e giu - - - - - ro, e giu - - - - -
25
ro di mai più, di mai più se - gui - re a - mor, mai più, mai più se - gui - re a - mor,

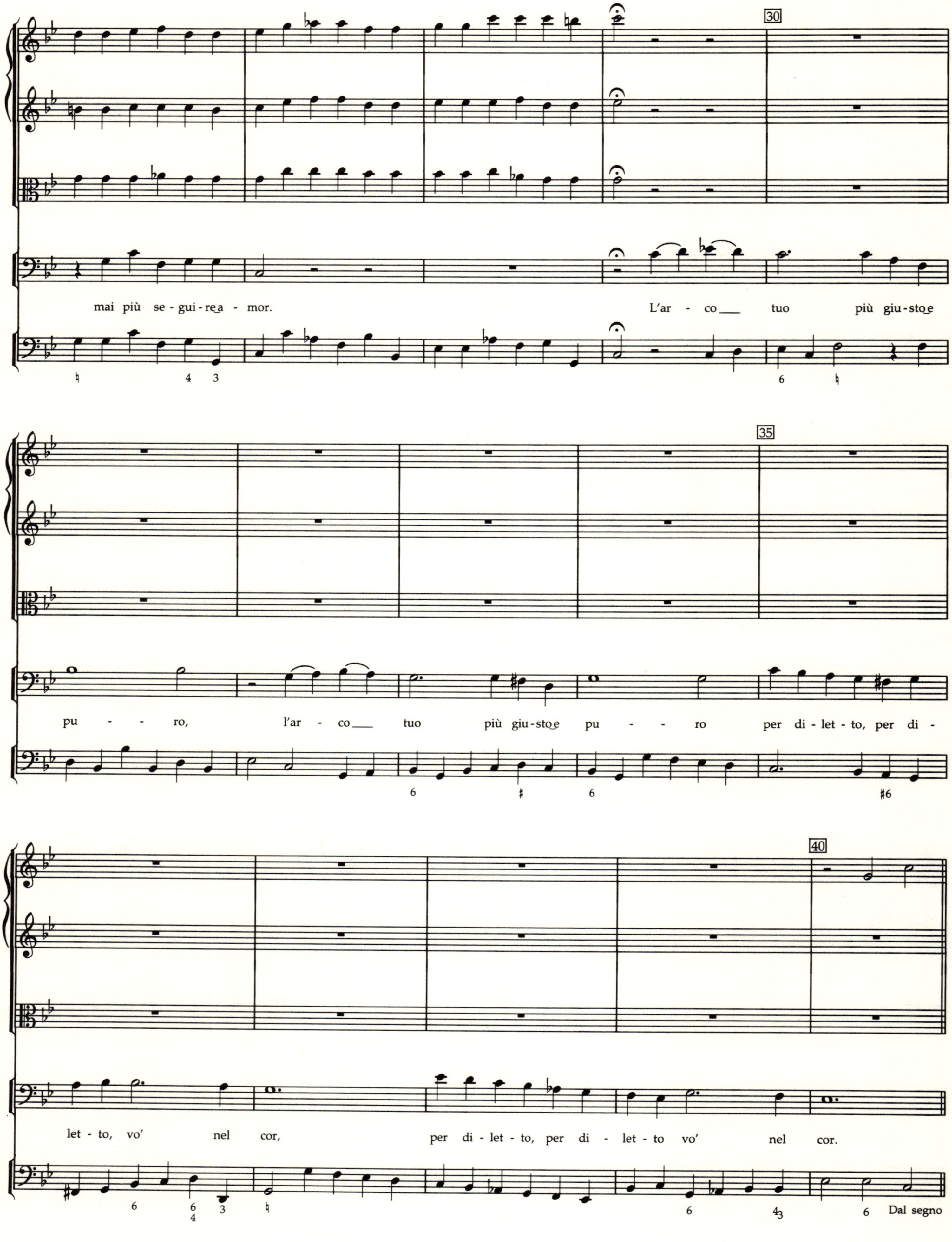
30
mai più se - gui - re a - mor.
L'ar - co tuo più giu - sto e
35
pu - ro, l'ar - co tuo più giu - sto e pu - ro per di - let - to, per di -
40
let - to, vo' nel cor, per di - let - to, per di - let - to vo' nel cor.
Dal segno

Scena xiv

Alessandro, Demetrio, Perinto, Apelle

105. *Recitativo*

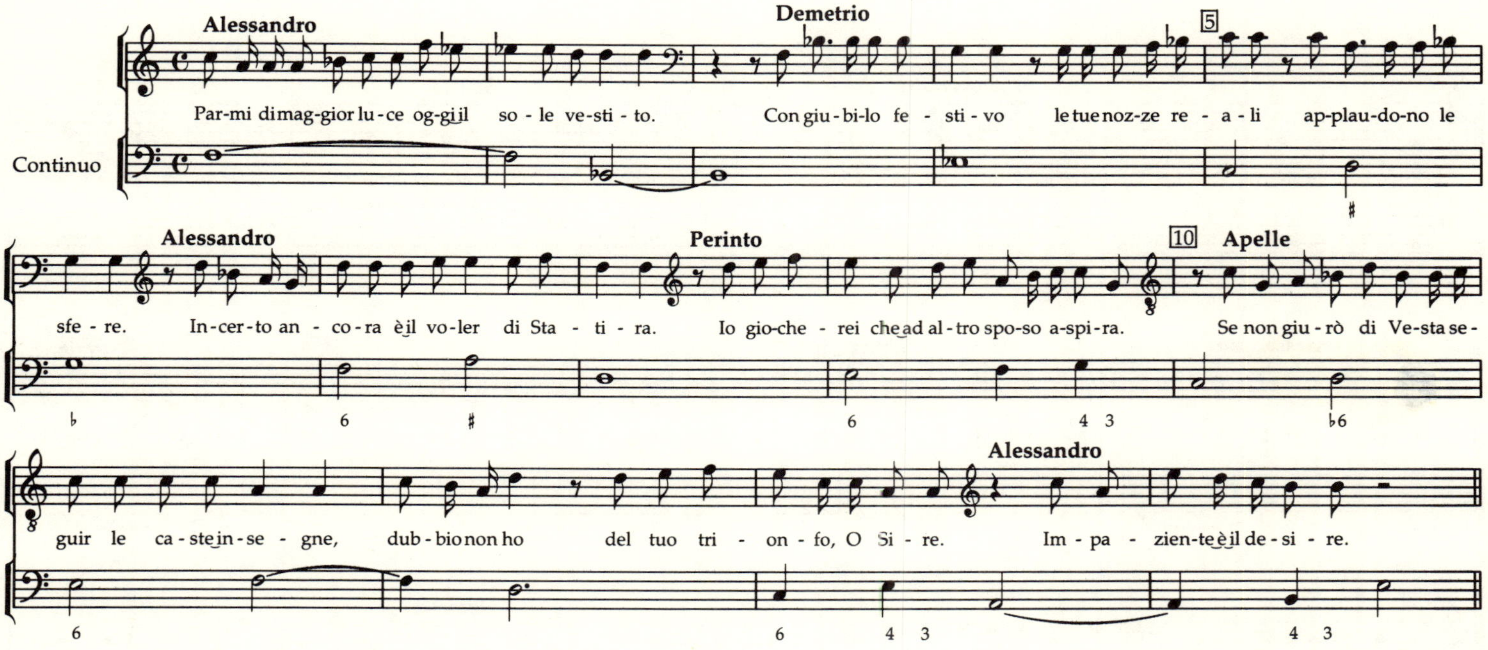

Scena xv

Statira, Oronte vestito all'eroica, Alessandro, Demetrio, Apelle, Perinto

106. *Recitativo*

Segue Statira l'aria con violini.

107. Aria

Grave
Violino I
Violino II
Viola
Statira
Continuo
p
Quel-la fè che mi giu-ra-sti è che mai tra-di-ta fu,
è che mai tra-di-ta fu. Quel-la al co-re de-sta a-mo-re se per sem-pre il cor le-ga-sti col va-lor di tua vir-
tù. Quel-la co-re de-sta a-mo-re col va-lor
solo
5
10

tutti
di tua vir - tù.
Quel - la fè che mi giu -
15
solo
p
ra - sti è che mai tra - di - ta fu, ma - - - - i tra - di - ta fu, mai tra - di - ta fu.

108. *Recitativo*

109. Aria

Allegro
Oronte
Continuo
Cor av - vez - zo a pian-ger
sem - pre mai non cre - de, mai non cre - de di gio - ir, a pian-ger sem - pre mai non cre - de, mai non
cre - de di gio - ir. Ben-chè ve - de da sua fe - de al - la sor - te can - giar
tem - pre, tie-ne an - cor vi - vo il mar - tir, vi - - - - - - - - - - vo il mar -
tir. Cor av - vez - zo a pian-ger sem - pre mai non cre - de, mai non cre - de di gio - ir, a pian-ger
sem - pre mai non cre - de, mai non cre - de di gio - ir.

110. Recitativo

Scena ultima

Alessandro, Statira, Oronte, Apelle, Demetrio,
Perinto e Campaspe che arriva e trattiene Alessandro.

111. *Recitativo*

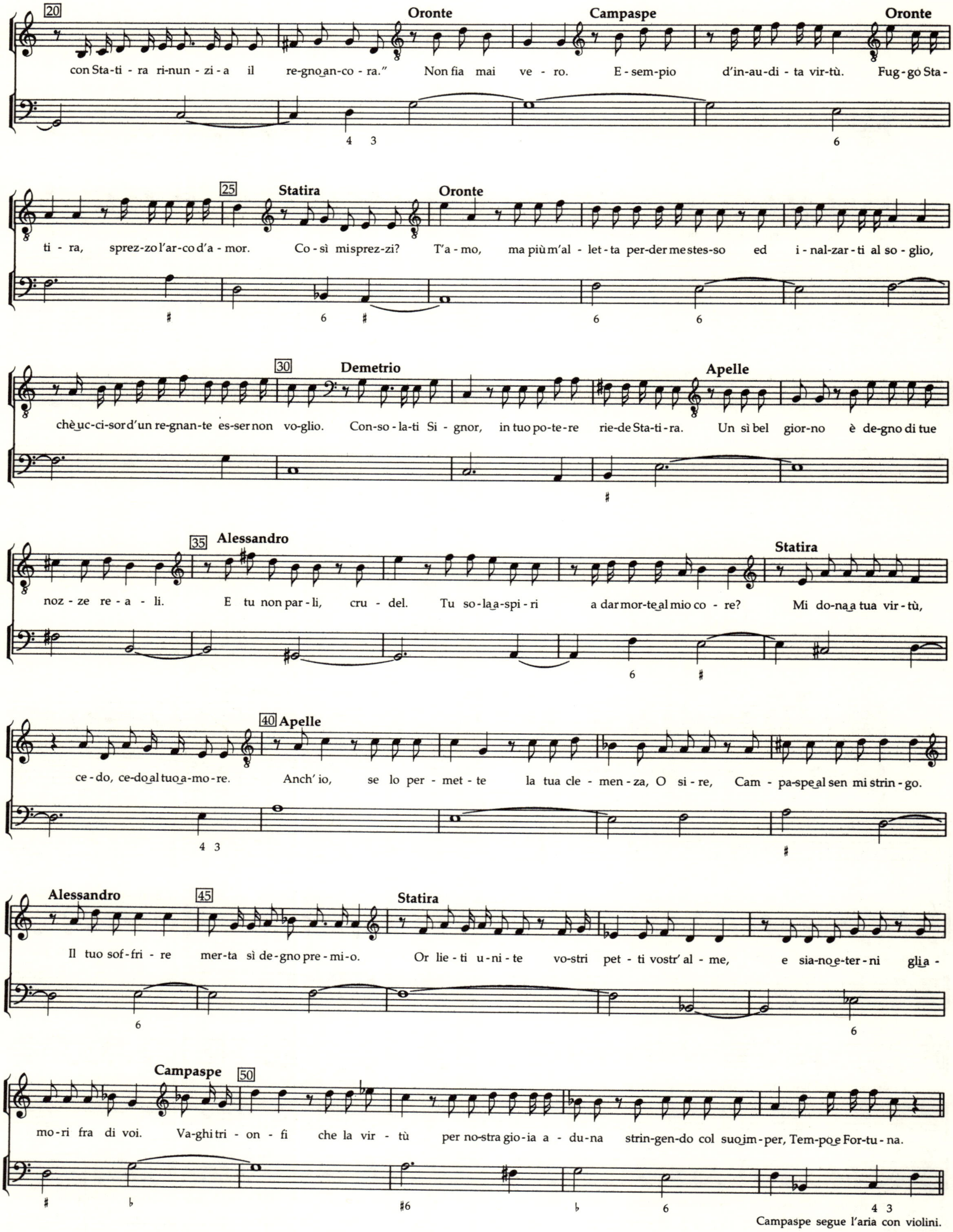

Campaspe segue l'aria con violini.

112. *Aria*

Allegro
Violino I
Violino II
Viola
Campaspe
Continuo
Se mi com-par-te il cie-lo o-re se-re-ne, se mi com-par-te il cie-lo o-re se-
5
re-ne, pian-ge-re più non vo', pian-ge-re più non vo' pian - - - - - - - ge-re più non vo', pian - -
10
- - - - ge-re più non vo'. Chè non con-vie - ne con in-dis-cre-to ze-lo, con in-dis-

15
p
p
p
p
cre-to ze-lo___ nu-dri-re quel-le pe - ne che_e-gli non de - sti-nò, quel-le pe - ne che_e-gli non de - sti - nò.
Da capo

Diana nella nuvola con
molti amorini intorno.

113. *Aria*

Andante
Diana
Continuo
Vi-va pur, vi-va pur l'ar-co_e gli stra - -
5
- - - - - - li dell' ar - cie - ro lu-sin-ghie - ro che col dar - do d'un bel guar - do sem-pre
fa col-pi fa-ta - - - - - - - - li,
10
dell' ar - cie-ro lu-sin-ghie-ro che col dar-do d'un bel guar-do sem-pre
fa col - pi fa - ta - - - - - li. Vi - va pur, vi - va pur l'ar - co_e gli stra - - -
15
- - - - - - - - - - - li, l'ar-co_e gli stra - - - - li.

114. *Recitativo*

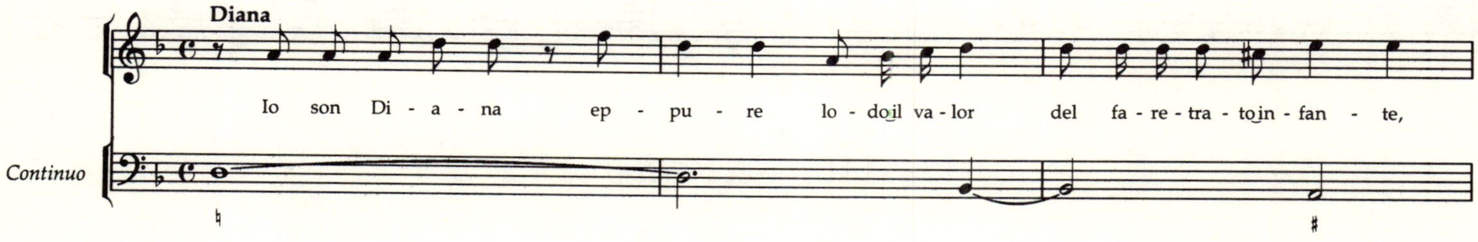

115. Aria

116. *Recitativo*

117. Aria

10
stes - so al mio duol ce-den - do op - pres - so col man - car la spe - me in
15
me, al mio duol ce-den - do op - pres - so col man - car la spe - me in me.
Da capo
Segue la 2ª Apelle.
Seconda stanza
20
Violino I
Violino II
Viola
Apelle
Continuo
Sì, sì, sì, che spi-ro per te sol, che spi-ro per te sol, per te, che

Fine dell' opera

APPENDIX

Two Arias from Naples, Conservatorio
di San Pietro a Majella,
M. 34.5.13

"Chi a volo troppo alto" (No. 58)

"Cor avvezzo" (No. 109)

58. Aria

INc, M. 34.5.13 f. 54v-58r

109. Aria

INc, M. 34.5.13 f. 101v-103v

di gio - ir, mai non cre - de, mai non cre - de, mai non cre - de
10
di gio - ir, non cre - - de di gio - ir. Ben - chè ve - de da sua fe - de al - la
15
20
sor - te can - giar tem - pre tie-ne an - cor vi - vo il mar - tir, vi - - - vo, vi - vo il mar - tir.
Da Capo

LA STATIRA

Libretto by
Pietro Ottoboni

(Rome, 1690)

Cast of Characters

Macedonians

Alessandro Magno, king of the Macedonians	[Soprano]
Campaspe, Alessandro's favorite	[Soprano]
Apelle, a painter who loves Campaspe	[Tenor]
Demetrio, general of the Macedonian army who also loves Campaspe	[Bass]
Perinto, a young servant of the court	[Soprano]

Persians

Statira, daughter of Dario, king of the Persians, who loves Oronte, but later becomes the wife of Alessandro	[Alto]
Oronte, Persian prince, who loves Statira and who is disguised as an Armenian merchant called Elvio	[Tenor]

Dances
of Persians
of Nymphs

The action takes place in and near Damascus.

Time: 333 B.C.

Changes of Scene

ACT I

Spacious countryside at night, with the moon
Dario's pavillion
Royal hall with statues
Prison where the remains of the Persian army are quartered, with soldiers seated upon their shields, and the remains of arms

ACT II

Picture gallery
Royal hall with statues
Mountain range with Statira's hut and the mausoleum of Dario

ACT III

Subterranean cavern
Forest which descends from Statira's hut to a valley
City square with triumphal arches and royal palace
Temple of Diana with victims on the altars

ACT I

Scene i

Open landscape, with a view in the distance of hills and tents, under which the Persian army is sleeping; starry sky with full moon.

ORONTE *alone*

2 ORON. Night, serene night, guardian of peace; how many brilliant stars shine in the heavens. They are the keepers of the promised calm. But for me, they do not have their usual power, because a heart in love does not know a minute of peace.

3 My constancy is of flint, I am of marble among torments; life gives me hope and I breathe with sighs. I do not yearn to be happy, chains are sweet to me; I do not refuse to suffer, and pain is a pleasure to me.

4 But what fierce noise of bellicose trumpets strikes my ears? Oh heavens, what do I see? The enemy in battle. Oh, there, warriors, quickly make ready your helmets and steeds.

Trumpets and the noise of people are heard.

Scene ii

All the hills are seen covered with the Macedonian army, which is marching slowly in the direction of the Persians. Alessandro is at the head of his soldiers, and Oronte is arousing the Persian camp.

5 ALES. Unconquerable warriors, at the sound of the trumpet fly on to punish; Fame is resounding on the crests of your helmets, and is handing you steel.

6 Now from the great mountains of Taurus you press forward your roots; now you hold the Persians in front, battle, and victory all in one. Mars and Bellona spread green laurel on your brow and make it a crown.

Alessandro throws himself into the midst of the enemy, and Oronte engages him in battle. After this there is a violent tussle. After lengthy combat, the Macedonians are victorious; they find Dario's beautiful chariot, put Alessandro in it, and present to him many bodies of the enemy.

7 ALES. Because, fond stars, you have given birth to my valor, you must cede to the sun the honor of clarifying such beautiful works. After Cintia, with her light, guided me to triumph, she hid herself and handed over my celebration to the blond goddess.

8 RITORNELLO. *Alessandro departs in the chariot drawn by Moors followed by many Persian soldiers.*

Scene iii

ORONTE *alone*

9 ORON. Cruel heavens, pitiless fate, iniquitous stars, you makers of ruins, filled with hate and anger; always rebels, you took the triumphal laurels from my brow replacing it with a loss. Cruel heavens, pitiless fate, iniquitous stars! King dead, honor lost; these are the furies of my heart, but a more harsh and bitter pain is the loss of his treasure. I have lost Statira and yet I do not die.

Scene iv

Dario's tent with a bed; Statira, kneeling by the body of her father, is crying.

STATIRA *alone*

STAT. Dario, my king, my father, my distress, do you abandon me thus? Thus do you leave Statira? 10

What tragic event to overcome my constancy do you 11
put to me, O gods? The kingdom is already lost, my father dead, his subjects overcome. And what hope is left for me, miserable princess, deprived of all my goods, steeped in grief? I shall enclose my feet in servile chains, my beauty will be but small food for a lascivious tyrant. Ah, unhappy fate, to end such pain, give me death.

Yes, I invoke death; death come to me. You only can 12
end all my trouble, and I shall know how to overcome the tricks of fortune with you.

Scene v

DEMETRIO *and* PERINTO *with soldiers;* STATIRA *on the bed in a melancholy attitude.*

PERI. I am not one of those champions so wild for 13
honor. Money delights me, I am the enemy of noise.

Look, sir, what a noble young woman is a prize for 14
you; she seems to me much more beautiful than the fair Campaspe.

DEME. The face of Campaspe is the image of the sun, alone among the stars and the most fair. Friends, with soft chains carefully bind the noble feet, and today take such a lovely captive to the ruler of the world.

Console yourself, do not cry so that you will be able 15
to thwart cruel destiny. The bow of the god of love which overcomes every heart could be formed by your hair.

STAT. The noble breast although pierced has made itself insensitive to grief. Perverse fate cannot overcome the soul with cruel bonds.

Sir, at least agree that my father not remain here un- 16
buried and prey to beasts. Lack of pity is no glory for you.

DEME. Is this perhaps Dario?

STAT. Precisely.

DEME. Such a great ruler merits every consideration; and you, royal one, excuse me if I do not release your feet from chains. I must do this and you must suffer.

PERI. I am of a rare and happy nature, nor do I lack 17
youth. I follow the sweet and not the bitter; I search for that which pleases me.

Scene vi

A royal hall.

CAMPASPE *alone*

CAMP. Here the great Alessandro full of victory placed 18
his head in my lap; here the warrior of Mars with quiet repose called forth the spirit of love. Love appears and wounds him; he laments, and tries to punish the audacious child. The quivered god flies elsewhere so that he, overcome, falls back on my breast.

A pleasing beauty gives warmth to a frozen heart. 19
Even the gods in heaven burn from this torch. A beautiful face shoots its arrow from the eyes; sweet arrow, harsh blow, mortal wound.

Scene vii

CAMPASPE, APELLE, *and* ORONTE *disguised as an Armenian*

20 APEL. I understand your situation, innocent Elvio, but fear not.

ORON. Fate brought me to Damascus. While Alessandro, the conqueror of the world, defeated Dario, I barely escaped with my life.

APEL. I shall take care of your safety.

ORON. Still . . .

APEL. What?

ORON. I sigh.

APEL. Liberty?

ORON. Not that.

APEL. Your lost riches?

ORON. My soul sighs only because I wish to be allowed to kneel before Statira.

APEL. That will be a difficult thing to accomplish.

ORON. And who will deny it to me?

APEL. It will be Alessandro, because he has already fallen in love with Statira, and today he wants to make her his wife and his queen.

CAMP. What do you mean, his wife and queen?

APEL. Excuse my lack of discretion, O fair Campaspe.

CAMP. Now, inform me which wife, which queen is destined for the breast of Alessandro.

APEL. It was the work of the clever thoughts of he who desires you. I praised the beauties of the lovely foreigner. Happily, with this new fire, Statira will go to him and Campaspe to me.

CAMP. What do I hear? These things are a sacrilege against the love and faith which you swore to me.

ORON. Fortunate discord! *to himself*

APEL. On the contrary, it is because I adore you that I do such things.

CAMP. Listen. From me, from my heart, expect vengeance and do not hope for love.

APEL. Why?

CAMP. I am now turned to stone against the person who will take the throne and crown from me.

APEL. I shall go to Alessandro in supplication; I shall speak of Campaspe; I shall reject Statira.

ORON. Sigh now, enamored heart. *to himself*

CAMP. Go now, only this will calm my anger and overcome the hate that engulfs me. Hope only for Virtue, Time, and Fortune.

21 Break your bow, blind god, if you do not have golden arrows. In my breast vile affection cannot strike a fatal blow. *Exit.*

Scene viii

22 ORON. Trust all to me, and if you are able to bring me into the presence of Statira, I promise to make you happy.

APEL. What can you do?

ORON. What you wish.

APEL. Oh, I cannot hope for anything.

ORON. That is an imprudent thought.

APEL. Tell me, then, how do you propose to make me happy?

ORON. You will soon see; I can say nothing more.

23 A wise heart never yields to grief, and it triumphs over fate. When a blue sky is smiling even a timid breast rejoices, and one can call strong only him who scorns the blond brow of fate. *Exit.*

Scene ix

APELLE *alone*

APEL. What is there left for me to hope for, if in order to win Campaspe I must allow her to go to another? I shall lose her to the king by remaining quiet. If I plead with her she is disdainful. Thus I lose her both by being quiet and by speaking. 24

I counsel myself with my heart and my heart is doubtful. Nothing is certain for me but the pain of lost liberty. I search in vain from my thoughts the manner to be happy, for both speaking and silence condemn me to suffer. 25

Scene x

Prison in the middle of which can be seen a tall catafalque with the body of Dario, his feet in chains; large numbers of Persian soldiers in chains; Statira in a black robe with a sorrowful expression.

STATIRA *alone*

STAT. Thus, O heavens, is a king treated, and you are the same ones who at other times threw down on the head of tyrants storms of just affliction. Is this the pomp and these the outrageous chains that comprise the obsequies of the Persian monarch? O inhuman Alessandro, cruel Demetrio, and even more, most cruel fate. Who taught you to tyrannize the dead, and to put in bonds she who to flee from you broke her heart? Eternal gods, I invoke you to punish the evil ones, and I only hope with my cries to render Jupiter severe. 26 27

Great thunder god, if the royal splendor carries the brilliance of your majesty, that affront which Dario receives must be punished by your arm. And it is just to be severe with him who rebels against you.

Scene xi

ALESSANDRO, DEMETRIO, *and* PERINTO; STATIRA *near the catafalque* 28

PERI. Sire, I promptly executed what Demetrio, your general ordered me to do. Here you see the cold body of Dario, and here you see his daughter. The vile remains of the Persian army, languishing in servitude, you see about you.

ALES. It is too sad.

DEME. Sire, it seems to me that such pride deserves such punishment.

ALES. Clemency and not anger prevails in me, for the greatest jewel that can crown the head of a victor is pity shown by the victor to the victim. 29

Clemency in the heart of a ruler is the true image of Apollo, because it does not burn flowers or plants but bathes them in quiet splendor. 30

STAT. If two royal bodies, one dead from pain and the other from the sword, awaken pity in you, then at my plea stop all this cruelty.

ALES. Excuse, O beautiful Statira, this involuntary error. To show you what a heart lies in this breast I release your chains and set your warriors free. Perinto, release their bonds, one by one.

PERI. Friends, be happy, what more do you desire? When you thought you were to die in servitude before, you can now walk freely. Friends, be happy.

STAT. Many, many thanks; my stupified mind does not know how to give you thanks. But if it does not weigh on you to be kind to one who begs you, Alessandro, do not deny me this kindness: I should like to pass the hours and the days in a remote forest, where the rays of Apollo never break the darkness, with the body of my father.

ALES. You abandon yourself too much to sorrow.

STAT. This is my wish.

ALES. Sometimes it is more virtuous to overcome one's self.

STAT. Pain not expressed by laments is not true pain.

ALES. I resolve to please you, and your virtue will counsel you how to scoff at Time and Fortune.

STAT. Thus you demonstrate, Alessandro, how justly the laurel leaves lie on your head.

31 Prepare yourselves, my eyes, to be happy to cry. Alone, I shall lament, nor shall I know how to breathe except in sorrow. *Exit.*

Scene xii

ALESSANDRO, DEMETRIO, PERINTO

32 ALES. On the banks of the Euphrates arises a solitary mountain. *To Demetrio* Demetrio, there is where I shall prepare a place for Statira.

DEME. Will you grant such a strange request, O Sire? Remember that your bed is lonely without a wife.

PERI. Decide, Sire, to take her for a wife, because you cannot find a more beautiful person.

DEME. Succumbing to your affection will be a victory.

ALES. Do as I say. It is my prerogative to provide succession in the kingdom with a marriage that both pleases you and is worthy of me. *Demetrio and Perinto leave.*

33 I do not yet know how to resolve this, to control my desires. I know how to overcome every assault, and I carry a breast of enamel against beauty. I still want to resist the knots of beautiful hair. It appears unjust to me to give my soul mockingly to the young god. *Exit.*

Scene xiii

A courtyard with some Persian soldiers.

DEMETRIO *and* PERINTO

34 DEME. In vain do I labor to instill desire for Statira in the royal heart, and the vain hope of obtaining my beloved Campaspe in this fashion seems to fly elsewhere.

PERI. You must not yet despair of the outcome. We shall dress the Armenian as a shepherd. And in the solitary cave he will exhort the foreign princess, Statira, to long for the royal bond. Thus she will return to court and entice Alessandro with her beauty. How does that seem to you?

DEME. I do not disdain prudent advice. I trust in you, Perinto, to evince sweet Cupid.

35 I want to hope for some favor from the god of love. It is not just that a faithful lover should weep forever.

Scene xiv

36 PERI. Persians, are you still delaying to take advantage of your fate? Arise, rejoice, throw away your bonds.

37 One must weep as little as possible, for the day is quickly fleeing. Once joy has left us, I believe that it will never return.

The dance of the Persian soldiers follows.

ACT II

Scene i

Picture gallery with portraits of Statira and Campaspe.

ALESSANDRO, APELLE

ALES. O Apelle, I saw Statira, I saw her and she is so like this portrait that between the two faces, one false, the other real, I cannot tell which is the most beautiful. 38

APEL. She certainly is beautiful, but the royal aspect of Campaspe, accustomed as it is to brilliant light, wisely matches the most beautiful one in the world to the most powerful.

ALES. I liked her once.

APEL. Is it that perhaps you do not care for her anymore?

ALES. Now there is the just fire of necessity burning in my breast.

APEL. Sire

ALES. What do you want?

APEL. I fear that the fire will not kindle in your great heart if Campaspe is not there.

ALES. You exalt her a great deal.

APEL. Oh Sire, I tell the truth.

ALES. Statira is of equal beauty, but because of her birth she prevails.

APEL. Excuse me, sir, what do you intend to do?

ALES. I am already resolved to raise her with me to the crown and the throne.

APEL. What will happen to the other?

ALES. She will be your wife.

APEL. In spite of joy my soul is still dubious.

ALES. APEL. *together* If I offend you, pardon me dear joy of my heart. One must blame that crude little god of love who, armed and naked, gives me pain. 39

Scene ii

CAMPASPE, ALESSANDRO, APELLE

CAMP. Covered with laurel and with Persians in chains you have added other realms to your kingdom. Sir, perhaps you come to me unusually late because your heart is so immersed in triumphs that you disdain my beauty which once you so desired. 40

I must hate your virtue as my rival if it forces the royal heart not to return to me. Thus your victories become my misery, for Mars ferociously disdains love. 41

ALES. It is my custom to vanquish the enemy phalanxes in the field. 42

CAMP. What do you mean?

ALES. That in this assault of love, by seeing you so late, my heart has won.

CAMP. Oh, my king, every mouth extols your victories. If you turn into a tyrant your honors and laurels will become tongues that speak of your cruelties.

ALES. It is prudence, not a fault, to overcome rebellious will.

APEL. One cannot call rebellious that spirit that urges us to welcome love and faithfulness in a heart. On the contrary, unjust is he who will not yield.

Can you be cruel to one who languishes for you? Is it worthwhile to be faithful without obtaining pity, without a reward? Cruelty to one who gives you his heart is not a virtue. *Exit.* 43

Scene iii

ALESSANDRO, CAMPASPE, STATIRA

44 STAT. Your having released my soldiers from chains, O Sire, having spared my life, and having felt pity for my misery, all these were actions worthy of you; but permitting me to pass quiet days in a solitary place surpasses all. You are worthy of the palms and if hidden tongues do not breathe your fame to eternity, I, in the forest, shall tell of your glory to the shepherds and the beasts.

ALES. Princess, I only fear that in following your desire I execute a tyrannical act.

CAMP. That pain is sweet, for if one desires something and the request is granted, it is called grace.

STAT. Beautiful one, I owe you much for your intercession.

CAMP. Thus is his plan not resolved and abandoned?

ALES. Statira, I owe you many favors, but . . .

STAT. But, do you not intend to grant this one?

ALES. I should first rather die.

STAT. I leave.

ALES. Not yet.

STAT. But why?

ALES. You give me pain, but this heart will resist and not give itself to vile love.

STAT. Then I may go?

ALES. Not yet, because the least you can do for this soul is not to leave.

CAMP. Tyrannical jealousy, you make me die.

STAT. You violate your agreement if you continue to resist.

ALES. You have won.

45 I shall suffer much pain to defend your honor, but this heart will resist and not give itself to vile love. *Exit.*

Scene iv

STATIRA, CAMPASPE

46 STAT. Without you, Campaspe, I should never have obtained his assent.

CAMP. Statira, the more that I think of that false faith in Alessandro's heart, the more I burn with anger and fury.

STAT. Then he once loved you?

CAMP. Here is the proof of it. *Shows her portrait.* This portrait that you see, the work of Apelle, he used to carry with him to his greatest battles; and when his enemies were defeated, he would return to this breast with honors and praises.

STAT. But I also see my portrait here.

CAMP. His heart is turning toward your beauty with new affection.

STAT. These attempts will be in vain, and if I remove myself from his eyes with quick steps, the new-born flame will be entombed, for the nourishment that feeds it will be lacking.

CAMP. This lifeless canvas will then go to war once more.

STAT. The adversary is in your power, and you can avenge without delay his wrongs.

CAMP. Imprudent one, you have not yet known the deceits of an unfaithful person, nor have you tried the poison of the god of Cnidus [Eros].

47 The lovers of today are liars and unstable. They give and take hearts by the thousand, and they always want to change their love. In this variable way they desire to enjoy more. *Exit.*

Scene v

STATIRA, ORONTE

STAT. What person known to me is approaching in foreign clothing? 48

ORON. I bow to you, adored eyes, my sun overcome by a disarmed and confused heart. The faithful lover, Oronte, inclines his head to his queen.

STAT. Prince, you arrive in time to give twofold happiness to my breast: I see you alive and I pray and desire your actions.

ORON. Command me.

STAT. That portrait that contains my features: you must take it and remove it from the eyes of the inflamed ruler.

ORON. O desired act! Hear, fair Statira, that once the Persian army was dispersed and fled, I saved my life in a small boat disguised as an Armenian. I know not how Apelle found me and defended me, for which my heart was grateful to him. I offered to repay him, and he, realizing that I am well-known to you, wishes me to take you far from the love of Alessandro.

STAT. And what does this have to do with him?

ORON. He adores Campaspe with noble sentiments. She wants to be on the throne, thus the greatest desire of this noble lover is to make his dearest one happy.

STAT. Fortune offers good occasion to follow virtue. You owe much to your friend, and I want to make Campaspe happy.

ORON. Then I shall steal the canvas without delay. *He detaches the portrait and hides it under his cloak.*

STAT. There among the high mountains where the Euphrates runs I go to enjoy alone an innocent life. I shall await you there, and you shall be my only comfort in my many unhappinesses.

Just god, kindle this soul of which thought is made a follower. I know how to scorn him who tries to betray the constancy of my breast with the magic of weak pleasure. *Exit.* 49

Scene vi

ORONTE *alone*

ORON. Among all of my misfortunes I still enjoy the gentle rays of some kind star. I owe you much Apelle, and since you are the reason that I am able to see my adored beloved, whatever I have within myself I give to your desires. My love is worth such a pleasure. 50

I am happy in my anguish even though I see the reason of my pain. Blind god of love, I want you in my breast; pull my chains even tighter. 51

Scene vii

Royal Hall. A large room in Campaspe's apartments with a huge float of flowers in the middle, everything decorated to resemble the kingdom of Flora. Campaspe seated upon the float, which is drawn by two white chargers, dressed as Flora, surrounded by many maidens representing the most notable flowers of the world. In the air, a number of little cupids who shower flowers on the stage.

ALESSANDRO, APELLE, CAMPASPE

ALES. How beautiful she seems to me. 52

APEL. The jealous woman will be wary of your attentions.

ALES. Majesty, happiness, and love have their throne in that face, and it appears that the archer of Cnidus [Eros] is more potent in her eyes.

APEL. Why, my lord, are you no longer faithful to her?
53 If that face pleases you, why are you so hard? She pants for you and only aspires to enjoy you in her loving breast and to awaken dead ardor.

54 CAMP. Let him who is able resist the arrow of love. Beauty does not look out for the one who has no feelings; for the one who seeks it, beauty gives his heart.
55 Return, return Alessandro to your former feelings; return to the breast of her who loves you. And if your great soul enjoys only triumphs, I, dressed as Flora, want to make you conqueror and lover.

ALES. I cannot deny that she is beautiful.

APEL. Worthy of your love.

ALES. Of all good fortune.

APEL. Campaspe, are you delaying to encircle your blond brow with palms? You have overcome your adversary.

CAMP. Is it really true, ungrateful heart, that you are returning to me? It is true that you are recalling your faith given falsely to your new loves? Ah yes, come, for from your cruel manner even a century of pain does not equal that sorrow which fills my breast.
56 I want to punish you, ungrateful one; I already know what I must do. I shall tell you of the madnesses this breast will try, and if you are not heartless you will be forced to weep.

57 ALES. I resolve to take her as my wife.

APEL. And what more just and beautiful action could Hymen bless?

CAMP. I shall be more than you expect: wife in your heart, servant at your side, warrior in your camp. In an instant I shall place myself in the bridal bed, shall give obeisance to the throne, and shall never fear the angry call of Mars.

ALES. And do you want to ignore Apelle's love like that? Do you thus leave the one who desires you more than his own life?

CAMP. My soul desires only Alessandro.

ALES. *To Apelle* And you, if you so love this beautiful tyrant, why do you want her bound to me eternally with such a strong bond?

APEL. So that my love might reign, I would not refuse death; such is the power of the affection that I have for her in my breast.

ALES. Your sincere feelings deserve to be rewarded; I give Campaspe to you.

CAMP.
APEL. Ah, this cannot be true!

ALES. Campaspe, you desire too much. It is quite enough to have a royal heart as a friend and not as a lover.
58 Whoever spreads his wings for too high a flight puts himself in danger of falling. Let discretion win over such a humble assault on the stars. *Exit.*

Scene viii

CAMPASPE, APELLE

59 CAMP. You for whom I have been forced to suffer so much, depart; go so far that in my rage I shall never see you again.

APEL. Because of your words. . . .

CAMP. He still speaks.

APEL. I resolve to die.

CAMP. Death is too lazy to take away your hated life; I cannot suffer you anymore. Leave.

APEL. I go to die, O heart of stone.
This is the reward given to my love, to my faith. Yes, 60
tyrant, I shall die and I shall give my soul as booty to the gentle breezes so that it might float around you. *Exit crying.*

Scene ix

DEMETRIO, CAMPASPE, PERINTO

DEME. My goddess. 61

CAMP. My comfort.

DEME. Such graciousness? *To himself*

CAMP. Thus I shall attain vengeance. *To herself*

DEME. If you were cruel before, suffering, now it seems to me, has made you kind to me.

CAMP. I am yours if you desire me, but . . .

DEME. What do you want me to do?

CAMP. My love will be the reward for your strength and your faith.

DEME. If the sole hope of possessing that which I so desire gives me the instruments, they will be deadly against anybody who has insulted you.

PERI. We are about to hear some bizarre command to miserable Demetrio.

CAMP. Once Statira arrived at this court, Alessandro fell in love with her. He wants her as his consort, and offends and insults me. I cry and assure him of the pain that torments me. He resists my laments even more strongly, and gives me as wife to Apelle.

DEME. And can you not break this union?

CAMP. You know well that once a royal hand joins two others by decree in this kingdom, they cannot be separated.

DEME. What is your command?

CAMP. Nothing but the death of both Apelle and Statira can break the bond, and release you from pain and me from obstacles.

DEME. I shall do it.

CAMP. And I await you, my dear, my breast burning with my love.
My disdained heart, prepare yourself. You furies of 62
hell, join with me. Now that I see my faith betrayed, come, lend your poison to me.

Scene x

PERINTO, DEMETRIO

PERI. In my opinion, what you are to do is monstrous. 63
Think about it well: women, often with twisted judgment, pull those who follow them over the precipice.

DEME. Any law of love, even though it seems doubtful or false, does not displease an inflamed heart.
I plead with you, my heart. Wild beasts, teach me, 64
show me the poison that you hide in your hearts. To follow love the mind must arm itself with fury.

Scene xi

A group of mountains with the hut of Statira and the mausoleum of Dario.

STATIRA *alone*

STAT. Now that I take solitary steps, far from court only 65
to venerate your soul; father, father, feel my sad torments. Listen to my plaints and console my desire. Only recently, and in a minute only, you were taken

from the blessed days that you wanted to consecrate to my happiness. Let sleep come to relieve my oppressed feelings and bring quiet peace. I give way to you, yes, I give way, blessed spirits, and I hope that in the shadows and in sleep at least you will guide my father to calm my breast.

66 Those sighs that disappear in the wind are grave in the surrounding air. They take the form of torment and return to me.

67 Thus, in my intense grief, I shall see my beloved father and departed spirits. There will finally be joy, but only in a dream.

68 *Orchestral ritornello. She rests against a large rock, and after the grave ritornello, she falls asleep.*

Scene xii

DEMETRIO, STATIRA *sleeping*

69 DEME. There she is; fate smiles on my act. Go, to the deed; courage; awaken, O cruelty. But what is taking away my heart?

STAT. Why are you so hard with me?

DEME. She speaks while dreaming.

STAT. Ah, crude Tricerberus, why do you oppose my desire?

DEME. She speaks of the underworld and foresees my blow. Campaspe, I consecrate the victim to your beautiful and serene face. Now I shall kill her. *He raises his hand to kill her.* Oh misery; how can I flee from the wrath of the angry heavens! *Demetrio flees as a violent earthquake begins, accompanied by thunder and lightening.*

Dance of nymphs in the forest.

ACT III

Scene i

Royal Hall.

ALESSANDRO *alone*

70 ALES. Tyrant, you try to dominate this soul once again. No, no, you will not win because you have not the strength to break down my heart.

71 Only one will obtain the glory of this soul. I am becoming mad from the pangs of love. Ah Campaspe, ah Statira, what a confused labyrinth I find myself in because of you. You have conquered the conqueror of the world.

72 I am overcome by the god of love. I kiss his bow and arrows that, aimed at the adored face of Statira, make mortal wounds.

Scene ii

Subterranean cavern.

APELLE *alone*

73 APEL. You flatter yourself and hope in vain to triumph over my constancy, O tyrant god of love. I have armed myself with a sword, and the face of death does not cast a shadow of horror over me.

74 I loved Campaspe, and I love her still. My faithful breast had never been kindled by another flame than that lovely being which Virtue has given force and power. But since she wants it thus, since the heavens, the earth, and the one I love want my anguish, let the heavens, the earth, and the one I love deal a severe blow against me. *He tries to kill himself, but is interrupted by Oronte.*

Scene iii

ORONTE, APELLE, *the voice of* CAMPASPE *offstage*

ORON. Friend, what disaster drives you to such lengths? 75

APEL. I must obey.

ORON. Whom?

APEL. Destiny.

ORON. A wise man keeps fate within bounds.

APEL. That is true, but a desperate man does not reason. Leave me.

ORON. What do you intend to do?

APEL. Put an end to my troubles.

ORON. Take hold of yourself.

APEL. You are doing nothing but prolonging my anguish.

ORON. Time gives good counsel.

APEL. Fortune disdains me.

ORON. Your character does not fear the pains of anguish. Do not do this, and put your life to better use.

CAMP. *offstage* Help, help!

ORON. That is a woman's voice.

APEL. One cannot yet distinguish from which direction it comes.

ORON. Let us hurry.

APEL. But where?

ORON. Here and there, until the reason for the screams is made known.

CAMP. *offstage* I am lost!

Scene iv

Campaspe enters trying to escape the claws of a lion. As she enters Apelle and Oronte fling themselves upon the beast and finally kill it.

CAMPASPE, APELLE, ORONTE

APEL. You, but . . . Oh God, Campaspe, my beloved. 76
You here alone. How is it that you are pursued by beasts, alone here in the forest, in caves?

CAMP. Your outraged heart will not look favorably upon the tears on my penitent face. But if pity reigns in your wise thoughts, I shall not despair of obtaining pardon.

I have offended you my love; I now ask pity. What I 77
was I am no longer, but I seek pity for my cruelty.

APEL. Are you mocking me still? 78

CAMP. No, I do not lie. After the terrible sentence made by me for your death, the painting of Statira was stolen from court. I knew that through this you were acting in my favor. Thus, confused by your virtue and overcome by my sorrow, wandering without help, hunting for you, fortune led me here to plead my defense.

ORON. Here is the portrait; I am guilty of the theft.

CAMP. Then Apelle did not take it?

ORON. I wished to satisfy the wishes of my friend, and was also opposed to the king's love for Statira; thus the canvas was taken.

CAMP. Am I then that ingrate, that vicious person who hated the lives of Apelle and Statira so much? Through my fault the innocent foreigner's life is in grave danger. Elvio, rush to her in order to stop this act.

ORON. Oh gods, what do I hear?

Please withhold your sharp knife, O Clotho, from 79

such a beautiful thread of life. Instead, turn your disdain on someone old. *Exit.*

CAMP. Unjust fate, do not try to steal such a beautiful flower. Feed your furor with less gracious food.

Scene v

CAMPASPE, APELLE

80 APEL. I must believe you, dearest, and banish all fear from my heart.

CAMP. Let your mind be at rest; I shall be yours only.

APEL. But the king?

CAMP. I don't care.

APEL. The throne?

CAMP. It is not important to me; it is better that it be Statira's.

APEL. And what gave you the desire to console me?

CAMP. Your faith.

81 Yes, yes, dear, I shall be yours. I shall give you tight bonds to possess my breast, and I shall never leave you.

82 APEL. Leave me, because heaven had condemned me to death. No longer do I wish to yield to the whims of fortune.

83 CAMP. Live, live for me, my sweet love.

APEL. Desire to obey you takes over my heart ever more forcefully. Here am I, either dead or alive, at your pleasure, for my life or my death is at your will.

84 Yes, yes, my beauty, come to me, and relieve all those pains by giving me that love by which I swear eternal faith.

85 CAMP. Leave me, O cruel one; I love you no more.

APEL. Dear one, no more of this.

CAMP. I feel again in my heart the flames for Alessandro, the ones you tried to kindle in this breast.

APEL. Oh, put an end to these pains, my love, and forget all pains in this breast.

CAMP.
APEL. *together* Peace, peace my wounded heart; think only to enjoy love. The young god is already triumphing, and all harshness is fleeing from my soul.

Scene vi

A forest that descends from the hut of Statira to a valley.

PERINTO *with soldiers*

87 PERI. The jealous king with good reason sends me to watch over his beautiful Statira, not because he fears some terrible pitfall for his beloved, but because she does not have devoted followers to care for her. But if he only knew what deeds cruel Demetrio plans, he then indeed would guard Statira.

88 There is no remedy; he who follows love never has happiness. Jealous tedium takes all peace from the heart.

Scene vii

Statira, supported by the arm of Oronte, comes down the mountain into the forest.

STATIRA, ORONTE, PERINTO *apart*

89 STAT. I cannot understand a thing.

ORON. Campaspe confessed to me that the greatest danger of a violent nature is imminent for you.

STAT. And who will attempt it?

ORON. That I do not know.

PERI. I know quite well, because I am from these parts.

STAT. Heaven will make the heart of the terrible traitor come to its senses. And you, Prince Oronte, if you come upon the wicked person, forget your anger and allow the gods in heaven their just vengeance.

PERI. Such unheard of pity! *To himself*

ORON. What clemency! But, madame, what armed people are approaching through the forest?

STAT. Greetings, friends, what person brings you here?

PERI. The king sends these archers to make your dwelling place more secure.

STAT. He honors me too much. Go to the king and tell him that I should like to speak with him.

PERI. I go immediately. *Exit.*

Scene viii

STATIRA, ORONTE, *later* DEMETRIO

STAT. Prince, I am still reflecting upon your news. 90

ORON. It is certain.

STAT. But what fault worthy of death does Campaspe see in me?

ORON. One day, jealousy of Alessandro led her to this, but now she repents her error.

STAT. Thus the killer of Statira will forever remain unknown to the world?

DEME. I shall not hide myself, royal lady, from your just ire. Behold the enemy, the murderer of Statira, that fury, that monster against whose barbarous desires the heavens, the earth, and hell burst forth. Yes, I am unworthy of pity.

My failings cause great danger to your great heart. Both clemency and harshness would like to take hold of them. 91

STAT. Who was the one that restrained you from your crime? Who was it who held back your hand from the unjust blow? 92

DEME. The heavens armed themselves to help you. As you were overcome with sweet sleep upon the rock, madame, I emerged from my place of ambush. I was about to deal the horrible blow when suddenly the sun disappeared, the earth trembled, the clouds, the mountains, and the plains cried out against me. They watched with disdain as I shuddered; then I, confused and weary, realized my error, and regretted my shameful act.

ORON. Demetrio, if Statira consents, I shall pardon you in her name.

STAT. Friend, you deserve every kindness, and my wishes will be ever with you.

To punish with favor is the best revenge of a royal soul. To win over a heart, such a weapon is better than all others. 93

Scene ix

A large square with triumphal arches and a royal palace in the background, its doors guarded, and many people in the windows.

ALESSANDRO, APELLE

ALES. Campaspe, then, showed pity toward you. 94

APEL. Sire, nothing more is required than your agreement.

ALES. Precisely. Today in the sacred temple you shall be married.

APEL. I give you thanks.

95 ALES. I am also perceiving gentle love. Love can be born from only a knowing glance. An unknowing glance never penetrates the heart. He who carries in his heart the wound of love, in order to give it refuge, sees it to be his love.

96 APEL. Sire, who will bring you pleasant news from your beloved?

ALES. Perinto. And it is precisely here that I await his arrival.

APEL. I counsel you that she should be received in the temple and not here.

ALES. I do not understand why.

APEL. There the gods, the altars, the priests, the impending sacrifice all serve as supports for your wishes, Sire; and if you find your beloved less hard, any delay might break the fatal knot.

ALES. That is a wise thought. Go there and enjoin the ministers of Diana such splendor of victims and incense as has never before been seen.

APEL. On such a beautiful day, in which the god of love triumphs, my breast is filled with joy.

97 The charming ray of hope gives an appearance of happiness to my sorrow. Pain is pleasure, and the chains given to me by blind love have lost their harshness.

Scene x

PERINTO *rushing in*, ALESSANDRO

98 PERI. Sire, Sire, the princess is already nearby; here come the servants that are rushing ahead of her.

ALES. Send Statira to the temple where I shall be awaiting her.

PERI. I obey. (And I understand you.) *To himself*

99 ALES. If my love is that sweet countenance for whom I break my heart, she will be welcomed in the temple by the loving victim. *Exit.*

Scene xi

PERINTO, CAMPASPE

100 PERI. Now is the time, by heaven, when Campaspe is no longer queen.

CAMP. What are you talking about? I no longer want the kingdom. I await only the faith of Apelle.

PERI. Wisely that which you cannot obtain, you modestly decline. But Demetrio?

CAMP. I detest him.

PERI. Even though you make great use of him in your desires.

CAMP. An unjust act, when it seems to lead to a desired end, deceives its followers and aids fate.

PERI. The crowd is already growing. *The crowd and the party of Statira grow ever larger.* To the temple, to the temple, my friends; there the king awaits you.

CAMP. I also desire to repent my error at the feet of the beautiful Statira.

PERI. You will find her of a sweet and kind heart, more willing to grant your prayers than to punish your errors.

CAMP. Then I have hope?

PERI. More than you might wish for.

CAMP. I shall go to her.

PERI. Have no doubts.

CAMP. I am confident.

Scene xii

Led by pages, halberdiers, muskateers, and a multitude of servants, Statira is seen in a gorgeous litter, from which, when it stops in the middle of the stage, she descends, attended by Oronte.

STATIRA, ORONTE, CAMPASPE, PERINTO

STAT. Oh there, stop here, and let my arrival be known 101
to the king.

PERI. O my lady, he awaits your graces in the temple.

STAT. And for what important reason does he remain there?

PERI. I cannot say. You will see such numbers of victims and unusual incense as to make the gods drunk with offerings.

STAT. Hasten the pace.

CAMP. And will Campaspe be left unpardoned for the grave unaccomplished error?

STAT. Arise, friend, and forget the unfortunate actions of the past. For you, I shall be as ready as are you to seek your good fortune.

CAMP. Oh graces which enchain the heart!

ORON. Nothing remains for you, beautiful Campaspe, except to enjoy happily the future with your beloved. It is only I who have no reason to hope.

STAT. You do not know yet, Prince, what the future holds for you. It is enough that you keep hoping.

In my breast I carry constant evidence of your sor- 102
rows. I throw forth the serenity of my countenance upon your anguish.

Scene xiii

Temple of Diana with the altar prepared for the sacrifice. A crowd of priests in the midst of which is a white stag, crowned with roses, as the victim.

DEMETRIO *alone*

DEME. Since I have turned my unbound feet far from 103
love, I enjoy freely the long-awaited breeze, as the living of a lover is dying yet remaining alive.

Chaste goddess, I vow and swear nevermore to fol- 104
low love. I want your just and pure bow for happiness in my heart.

Scene xiv

ALESSANDRO, DEMETRIO, PERINTO, APELLE

ALES. Today it seems to me that the sun shines brighter. 105

DEME. The spheres are applauding your royal marriage with festive exaltation.

ALES. Statira's will is as yet uncertain.

PERI. I'll bet that she desires another husband. *Aside*

APEL. If she has not sworn to follow the chaste teaching of Vesta, I have no doubt of your triumph, Sire.

ALES. Desire is impatient.

Scene xv

STATIRA, ORONTE, *dressed in a heroic manner*, ALESSANDRO, DEMETRIO, APELLE, PERINTO

STAT. Statira humbly bows to your sovereign visage. 106

ALES. Madame, to whose virtue Alessandro's soul by force is overcome and yields, I have nothing in my power that can be far from your wish.

STAT. A strange command from my father spurs me to ask a husband from you. He appeared in a dream, and thus he spoke, "Leave the hut, my daughter, grieve no more, go to the court where a noble consort will take away these dark shades from your heart. Heaven wills it thus." And saying that, he disappeared.

ALES. Did he name the person, or did he give you an inclination for marriage?

STAT. It is precisely this inclination that guides me and counsels me.

ALES. Explain then, whom do you desire in your heart?

STAT. But you, Sire, will you decline my desire?

ALES. I pledge my royal word.

STAT. Even though the chosen one would not be acceptable to you?

APEL. With pure and noble pretexts she sweetly torments the anxious sovereign.

DEME. And she makes the wound to the heart sweeter.

PERI. We shall soon see.

ALES. Resolve it, then, beautiful one, and let not your desire remain unknown.

STAT. Do you trust me?

ALES. Do not doubt it.

STAT. This is your word?

ALES. It is the law.

PERI. The priests here in the temple have the victims prepared to celebrate the marriage.

ALES. You still delay?

STAT. I obey, and I shall marry Oronte.

APEL. DEME. *together* Unexpected event!

ORON. You raise me up too much.

107 STAT. The king has already agreed. That faith you swore to me was never betrayed. It excites love in a heart if you join forever that heart with the worth of your virtue.

108 Under false garments, Sire, this person is Prince Oronte of Persia. He, in order never to be far from my side, disguised himself as an Armenian. Thus if I open my breast to the love he professes for me, I give him little, although I give him myself.

ORON. Excuse me, invincible monarch, if I hid my name, my country, and my thoughts from you; the young god of love is responsible for it.

STAT. The troth is already pledged, and it remains only for you to confirm it, Sire.

ALES. In order that my wishes be known, you will soon read my thoughts.

DEME. The king seems distraught.

APEL. Perhaps he does not like the unexpected decision of Statira.

PERI. If he really loves her, he can well force her to be his wife.

ORON. My soul does not dare wish for such pleasure.

109 My heart, accustomed always to weep, will never believe in happiness. Even though it sees, because of faith, fortune changing its hardness, my heart's anguish remains alive.

110 ALES. Here is the written document. Statira, enjoy your faithful husband in happiness.

STAT. ORON. *together* My senses are confused by such kindnesses.

ALES. Necessity leads me elsewhere. Goodbye.

STAT. The king departs thus?

Scene xvi

ALESSANDRO, STATIRA, ORONTE, APELLE, DEMETRIO, PERINTO, *and* CAMPASPE *who enters and stops Alessandro*

CAMP. Stop, most revered ruler. 111

ALES. To whom are you speaking?

CAMP. To you.

ALES. I am no longer king, for I have given Statira to Oronte, and with her the kingdom.

STAT. ORON. *together* Oh, my heart is confused!

ALES. Cruel pledge.

STAT. Let me read the letter and translate from writing to speech what decree the king lays down. "Since Statira gives herself as wife to Oronte, my soul that does not die in seeing its love ignored, cedes her to my rival. Indeed, to demonstrate how much I adore her, with Statira I also renounce the throne."

ORON. But this cannot be true.

CAMP. An example of unheard-of virtue.

ORON. I am leaving, Statira. I scorn the bow of love.

STAT. Thus you scorn me?

ORON. I love you, but it is better to leave and raise you to the throne; I do not want to be the murderer of a monarch.

DEME. Console yourself, Sire, Statira returns to your power.

APEL. Such a beautiful day is worthy of your royal wedding.

ALES. You do not speak, cruel one. Is it only you who wishes to give death to my heart?

STAT. I give myself to your virtue; I yield to your love.

APEL. Sire, if your clemency permits it, I shall also clasp Campaspe to my breast.

ALES. Your suffering merits such a worthy prize.

STAT. Then unite your breasts, your souls, and let there be eternal love between you.

CAMP. O sweet triumphs that Virtue gathers for our joy, clasping with its authority both Time and Fortune.

Because heaven bestows on me peaceful times, I do 112
not want to grieve anymore. It is not proper to nurture, with indiscreet zeal, those pains which heaven destined.

DIANA *on a cloud surrounded by many little cupids*

DIAN. Long live the bow and arrows of the sweet little 113
archer, who with the shot of a sweet glance always makes fatal wounds.

I am Diana; I praise the worth of the little god, and I 114
am the lover of Love.

The great soul will incite the sweet envy of all the 115
gods when heaven will learn today of the victory of the two blessed spirits.

STAT. Now I am at your command, Alessandro; come 116
and take away all care from my breast.

ALES. I live only for you. Yes, I live only for you. I 117
thought I was lost to my anguish, languishing and oppressed by the lack of hope.

APEL. Yes, I breathe only for you; destiny wants me happy; hoping, I did not fail to triumph over my pain.

The End